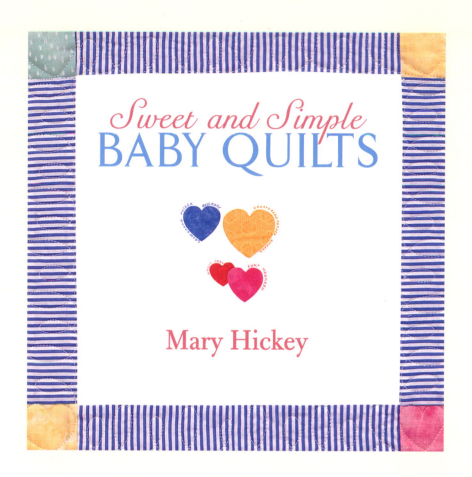

Sweet and Simple
BABY QUILTS

Mary Hickey

Martingale™
& COMPANY

Sweet and Simple Baby Quilts
© 2003 by Mary Hickey

& COMPANY

That Patchwork Place®

That Patchwork Place® is an imprint of
Martingale & Company™.

Martingale & Company
20205 144th Avenue NE
Woodinville, WA 98072-8478 USA
www.martingale-pub.com

CREDITS

President . . . . Nancy J. Martin
CEO . . . . Daniel J. Martin
Publisher . . . . Jane Hamada
Editorial Director . . . . Mary V. Green
Managing Editor . . . . Tina Cook
Technical Editor . . . . Ellen Pahl
Copy Editor . . . . Melissa Bryan
Design Director . . . . Stan Green
Illustrator . . . . Laurel Strand
Cover Designer . . . . Regina Girard
Text Designer . . . . Stan Green
Photographer . . . . Brent Kane

Printed in China

08 07 06 05 04 03   8 7 6 5 4 3 2 1

DEDICATED TO JOSH, RIKKI, AND AUDREY

Library of Congress Cataloging-in-Publication Data

Hickey, Mary.
    Sweet and simple baby quilts / Mary Hickey.
        p. cm.
    ISBN 1-56477-426-0
    1. Quilting—Patterns. 2. Patchwork—Patterns.
3. Children's quilts. I. Title.

    TT835 .H4545 2002
    746.46'041—dc21   2002151279

CONTENTS

◈ INTRODUCTION

AT THE HEART OF BEING A WOMAN is the drive to nurture and shelter those we care for, especially little ones. Quilting provides an outlet for this drive in many ways. Of course, first and foremost, quilts keep babies warm. More than that though, making a quilt allows us to peek ahead to share our dreams for the baby and express love, affection, and caring—often even before the baby is born. Making quilts for my own first grandchild, Audrey, has given me a wealth of inspiration for blocks, settings, and colors for baby quilts and has given me a chance to channel the energy from the huge flood of love I feel for her. I think of a baby quilt as a wrapping of love that conveys a message of tenderness and devotion. Stitching a quilt for a baby is an opportunity to create something of lasting beauty, which can carry our message of love and warmth into the future as the child grows.

The quilts in this book were designed to be easy to make, straightforward, and uncomplicated. If you are making your first quilt or if you are an experienced quiltmaker who needs to whip up a quick project, then one of the quilts in the first part of the book would be a good choice: "Cobblestones," "Pink Lemonade," "Wonder Baby," "Baby Bow Ties," "Bright Garden," "Petite Bouquets," and "Little Buddy" are exceptionally quick and easy. If you have an irresistible novelty or conversation print, consider making "Baby Buckaroos" or "Playmates" because these are also very simple quilts and highlight special fabrics or novelty prints.

"Family Hearts" and "Wiggle Flowers" are both easy appliqué quilts and good choices if you like appliqué or are not that comfortable with machine piecing. Both lend themselves to all types of appliqué—hand, machine, or fusible.

The other quilts in the book—"Sunny Sailors," "Baby Baskets," "Pipsqueak Picnic," "Evening Stars," and "Topsy Turvy Hearts"—look complex but are actually easy and include remarkably clever construction methods. For example, "Pipsqueak Picnic" on page 84 may have many pieces and lots of triangles, but all the patches start out as simple squares and rectangles; you never have to cut or hold a triangle to make the quilt. If you look at "Topsy Turvy Hearts" on page 92, you'll see stars peeking out among the hearts, but you never have to piece a star block. All the quilts provide an opportunity to play with color, light, pattern, and rhythm, and to send a message of loving welcome to a new baby.

Feel free to add your own personal touch to the quilt projects. Your personality and individual creativity, the work of your own hands, will transform any quilt into your own small masterpiece to send into the future.

Enjoy the quilts, and the babies!

Mary Hickey

♥♥♥ QUILTING ABCs

QUILTS CONSIST OF THREE LAYERS stitched together to create a coverlet for warmth or a work of art. The three layers are the top, the batting, and the backing.

The top layer of the quilt is the part we enjoy making with pieced blocks or with designs appliquéd to a background fabric. This book includes instructions for making both pieced and appliquéd blocks.

The middle of a quilt is usually made of a fluffy material called batting. For baby quilts, I usually like a cotton batting. It has a nice soft feel, an old-fashioned look, and it gets softer with every washing.

The back, or backing, of the quilt is the third layer. It can be very simple, consisting of a single piece of plain fabric, or it can be more complex with beautiful fabrics or more piecing. The three layers are held together by "quilting" stitches. Quilting can be done by hand or machine; it can be very simple or very complex. It always adds soft shaping, sculpting, and dimension to the quilt.

In this part of the book, I'll walk you through the process of quiltmaking, from start to finish.

🧺 FABRICS

CHOOSING FABRICS FOR A BABY quilt is easy and fun. You need only small pieces of fabric and you can be a little wild with the colors if you want. Be sure to use only 100% cotton fabrics for baby quilts. To choose the fabrics for a successful baby quilt, I suggest using one of these simple strategies:

♥ Theme or conversation prints

♥ Nursery colors

♥ Colors you simply like

♥ Multicolors or primary colors

Theme or Conversation Prints

Theme, or "conversation," prints are just that—printed fabrics based on a theme or consisting of small images. Choose one fun fabric that you really want to work with. Then look at the colors in that fabric and pick a few of those for the rest of the quilt. Or, choose one color in the print and use several shades of that color.

For example, the fabric in "Playmates" on page 60 features a little girl in a pink dress. I used that same pink plus a darker one and a lighter one. This creates a lovely frame around the children and makes a traditional-style quilt. The same technique makes "Baby Buckaroos" on page 38 irresistible with three shades of blue. The quilts look complex but are really very easy. Notice that in the "Wonder Baby" quilt on page 34, the key fabric is the pastel dot used in the setting squares and the outer border. Simply echoing the dot colors in the Four Patch blocks made color selection a breeze. Any novelty or conversation print will work for this quilt.

"Playmates" Block

"Baby Buckaroos" Block

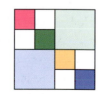

"Wonder Baby" Block

TO USE OR NOT TO USE

Many times, new mothers receive a beautiful baby quilt and want to keep it as a family heirloom; they don't let their babies actually use the quilt. When I make an heirloom-quality quilt, I always feel that I need to make a second little quilt for the baby—to be the official "blankie!" So I make the honored quilt for the ages, usually in the chosen nursery colors, such as "Baby Baskets" on page 78. But then I whip up a second quilt that is quick and easy to sew. "Little Buddy" on page 56, "Playmates" on page 60, and "Baby Bow Ties" on page 42 are all perfect for dragging, drooling, and serious cuddling.

Nursery Colors

The nursery colors often determine the color scheme of a baby quilt. I usually repeat the two main colors of the nursery, using several shades of these colors. Then I add a third color based on a combination of the mother's preferences and the shades that combine well with the main colors. To keep baby quilts light and fresh, I like to use a bit of white or cream as well.

When I made "Baby Baskets," shown on page 78, it was in the nursery colors of pale peach with white woodwork. We settled on green as the third color since blue-green is the compliment of peach (red-orange) on the color wheel. I made the quilt with several shades of green and peach plus a bit of white.

"Sunny Sailors," shown on page 74, was made for a baby whose nursery was a pale blue, so light that it was almost white. We could easily have made the quilt red, white, and blue, but since the baby's room was on the north side of the house in the shadow of the porch, I decided to use yellow instead to bring some sunshine into the room. Blue and yellow create a cheerful atmosphere, and the white sails added a bit of fresh air to the quilt.

"Baby Baskets" Block

"Sunny Sailors" Block

Colors You Simply Like

You can also choose a color scheme just because you would like to work with it. For example, "Evening Stars" on page 88 is the simple combination of pastel blues and greens that I find soothing. "Sunny Sailors" on page 74 is blue and yellow, always a winning combination. A baby quilt can also be a chance to play and experiment with colors or work with colors outside your comfort zone.

"Evening Stars" Blocks

"Sunny Sailors" Block

Multicolors or Primary Colors

When I have no real color scheme in mind and I am not using a theme print, I often make the quilt out of a variety of colors, especially two shades of the four primaries, such as red, green, blue, and yellow. "Bright Garden" on page 46 is done in red, yellow, blue, and green. Bright colors are always fun to stitch.

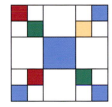

"Bright Garden" Block

PREWASHING FABRICS

All fabrics destined for your sewing room must stop and visit the washing machine and dryer first. Because you are working with 100% cotton fabrics, the fabrics should be preshrunk and the excess dye must be washed out. Prewashing also removes chemicals and sizing added to fabrics in the manufacturing process. Wash darks and lights separately in warm water in your washing machine. Tumble dry in a warm dryer.

TOOLS OF THE TRADE

THERE ARE SOME BASIC ESSENTIALS you'll need for quiltmaking. Buy the best tools you can afford. Your investment in quality tools and supplies will pay off in the long run.

Cutting Tools

Good rotary-cutting equipment allows you to cut quickly and accurately. If you do not have rotary-cutting equipment, start by purchasing a cutter with a 2" blade. Check the instructions that come with it to learn the proper way to hold it and how to use the safety guard. You will also need a cutting mat on which to cut. An 18" x 24" mat is a good all-purpose size. Rotary-cutting rulers are ⅛"-thick acrylic, enabling you to guide the rotary cutter next to it. The 6" x 24" size is the most essential. I also find that a 6" Bias Square® ruler is indispensable.

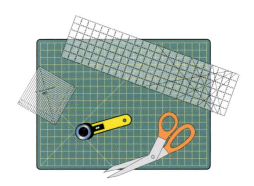

I recommend having two pairs of good-quality scissors—a large pair for cutting fabric and a small pair for cutting appliqué pieces and thread. Do not cut anything but fabric or thread with them.

Sewing Machine

A nice straight-stitch machine in good working order will do just about everything you need to make quilts. Take the time to get to know your machine: how it is threaded, how the functions work, and how to keep it oiled properly.

Two useful attachments for your machine are a walking foot, which helps feed thick layers of a quilt through your machine more evenly when attaching bindings or machine quilting, and a darning foot for free-motion machine quilting.

Walking Foot   Darning Foot

Needles

Replace the needles in your sewing machine regularly. An 80/12 is just right for machine piecing. For handwork, use a size 10 or 11 "Sharp" for hand appliqué and a size 7 or 8 "Between" for hand quilting.

Pins

Steel straight pins with glass or plastic heads are handy for most pinning jobs. If pins are extremely thin and you sew slowly, you can leave them in place while machine sewing. Safety pins are used for basting layers of the quilt together for machine quilting.

Mary's Helpful Hint

Use a separate magnetic pin holder for each type of pin.

Iron

Look for a steam iron that produces plenty of steam. Some quilters like the ones that shut themselves off if they haven't been used in a while. Others like an iron that stays hot all day.

CUTTING AND PIECING YOUR QUILT

QUILTMAKERS HAVE DEVISED A VARIETY of clever strip-cutting and piecing techniques to use with rotary equipment. Who would ever guess that "Pink Lemonade" Nine Patch blocks (page 30) would be made from three long strips of fabric first sewn into a strip unit and then cut to make the little squares? And who could imagine that "Pipsqueak Picnic" (page 84) with all its little triangles could be made without ever cutting or holding a triangle in your hands? Yes, what we quilters really like is putting a little masterpiece in a pretty box with tissue and ribbons and having friends at the shower think that we are quilting goddesses who spend thousands of hours slaving away out of love and devotion. Little do they know that we zoom along with our rotary cutters and strips, sew a quilt quickly, and have a great time doing it!

Rotary Cutting Strips

Whether you are a beginner or an old pro, always follow a few precautions when rotary cutting. The rotary blade is extremely sharp, and before you notice, you can unintentionally cut something important, such as your finger. Make the following safety rules a habit.

♥ Always push the blade guard into place whenever you finish your cut. Keep the nut tight enough so that the guard won't slide back unintentionally.

♥ If you have small children (under age 20), keep your cutter in a safe place when not in use.

♥ Always roll the cutter away from you.

THE CLEANUP CUT

Cutting strips at an exact right angle to the folded edge of your fabric is the foundation for accuracy. Start with the first cut, known as the cleanup cut.

    Fold your prewashed fabric in half with the selvages together, and press. Place the fabric on your cutting mat with the folded edge closest to you. Align the fold with the horizontal lines on the cutting mat. Place a 6" x 24" acrylic ruler so that the raw edges of both layers of fabric are covered and the lines of your ruler match up with the vertical grid on your mat. Hold the ruler steady with your left hand. Rolling the cutter away from you, cut along the edge of it from the fold to the selvages. Remove the ruler and gently remove the waste strip.

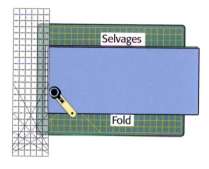

CUTTING STRIPS

To cut strips, align the desired strip width on the ruler with the cut edge of the fabric. After cutting three or four strips, realign the fold of your fabric with the lines on your mat and make a new cleanup cut.

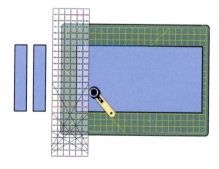

CUTTING SQUARES AND RECTANGLES

To cut squares and rectangles, cut strips in the desired widths. Cut the selvage ends off the strip. Align the required measurements on the ruler with the left edge

of the strip and cut a square or rectangle. Continue cutting until you have the required number of pieces. Use your ruler and periodically check that your piece measurements are accurate.

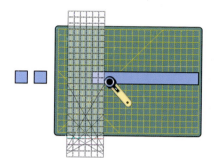

CUTTING SPECIAL MOTIFS: "FUSSY CUTTING"

We are fortunate to live in an era when hundreds of adorable novelty or conversation prints are available. Two or three quilts in this book were planned specifically to use these prints successfully. Many baby quilts contain a square in which you can feature a novelty or conversation print.

Look for a quilt block design that has a large open area where you can effectively use a little printed scene or motif. The Snowball block is my favorite. Then find another block to alternate with the Snowball block, such as a Nine Patch or an Hourglass block.

If the motifs of the novelty print are close together and evenly spaced (which almost never happens), you can cut strips across the fabric width and then crosscut the strip into squares. If the motifs are unevenly spaced, you will need to selectively cut, or "fussy cut," the motifs. I had to do this to cut squares from the bouquet fabric in "Petite Bouquets" on page 52. "Baby Buckaroos" on page 38, "Playmates" on page 60, and "Pipsqueak Picnic" on page 84 also required some fussy cutting.

A 6" or 12" square ruler is useful for fussy cutting. If you are cutting many squares, place masking tape on the ruler along the appropriate markings.

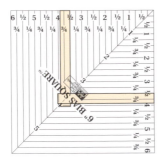

Move the marked ruler around the fabric to isolate a motif. Cut the first two sides. Next, turn the ruler around and align the desired markings with the just-cut edges. Cut the remaining two sides. If you have a limited amount of fabric, you might want to plan all your cuts first by using a pencil or a blue water-soluble pen to draw the cutting lines.

Cut the first two sides.

Sewing

Now for the fun part—sitting down to sew. Make sure you have a comfortable chair and good light.

STITCH LENGTH

Set the stitch length dial on your sewing machine to about 12 stitches per inch (2.5 on many machines). When blocks are sewn directly to other blocks without sashing, the seams often need to be pinned or basted. For machine basting, set the stitch length to 6 stitches per inch.

THE ¼" SEAM ALLOWANCE

All the measurements for the quilts in this book are based on using an exact ¼" seam allowance. You might be able to purchase a special ¼" presser foot for your machine. You can use the edge of the presser foot to guide the edge of the fabric for a perfect ¼" seam allowance. If you do not have a ¼" foot for your machine, take a few minutes to establish an exact ¼" seam guide on your machine.

1. Place your ruler or a piece of graph paper with four squares to the inch under the presser foot. Slide it around until you have the needle directly above the ¼" line on the right-hand side of the ruler or paper. Gently lower the needle until it sits precisely on that ¼" line.

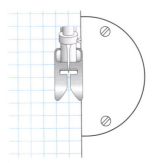

2. Make a thick guide by layering 5 strips of ¾" or 1" masking tape on your cutting mat (one piece right on top of the other).

3. Look at the area to the right of the ruler or graph paper, which is still under your needle and presser foot. If the feed dogs of your machine extend out to the right of the presser foot, use a pencil to draw a notch on the masking tape guide. Draw the notch about the same size as the exposed feed dogs. Use paper scissors to cut away the notch area.

4. Using the ruler or graph paper as a guide, lay the masking tape on the deck of the sewing machine so that the uncut edge of the masking tape is aligned to the exact right of the ruler or graph paper.

5. The guide is the portion of the tape without the notch. Because the tape is very thick, you will find it easy to keep the fabric on track.

Chain Piecing

After perfecting the ¼" seam, organize yourself with the same discipline as an Olympic athlete—prepare for a sewing marathon! Align the two fabrics you will be stitching and place them under the presser foot. Lower the presser foot and place your right hand behind the needle, holding on to the two threads. Continue to hold on to the threads while the machine sews the first few stitches.

When you have sewn the first pair of pieces or strips, leave them in the machine and feed the next pair in without removing the first pair. This will save you much time and thread. Organize all the pieces that are to be joined right sides together. Arrange them in a stack with the side to be sewn on the right.

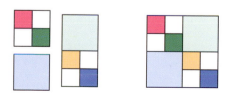

Chain Piecing

Making Blocks

The instructions and illustrations for each quilt project show you the steps in which to join the pieces of your block. In general, the shortest seams will be sewn first and you will sew progressively longer straight lines. Practice looking at quilt block designs to see if any section can be sewn as a unit first and then cut. If you can sew and press before cutting, you eliminate two opportunities to distort a shape after you have cut it.

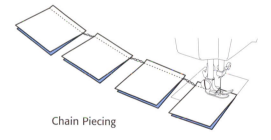

Many wonderful quilt blocks are made up of squares. If you had to cut out 200 squares, one at a time, and then sew each one to the next, the project would seem daunting. But think about cutting long strips of each fabric, sewing them together, and then cutting across them to make segments or units of squares already sewn together. These are called strip sets, and they are a quick and efficient way of cutting and piecing many blocks and block units.

After sewing strips together, do a cleanup cut to remove the selvage ends of the strip set. Align the required measurement on the ruler with the cleanly cut left edge of the strip set and cut the specified number of segments. Often you will stitch the segments to other segments to make Four Patch or Nine Patch blocks.

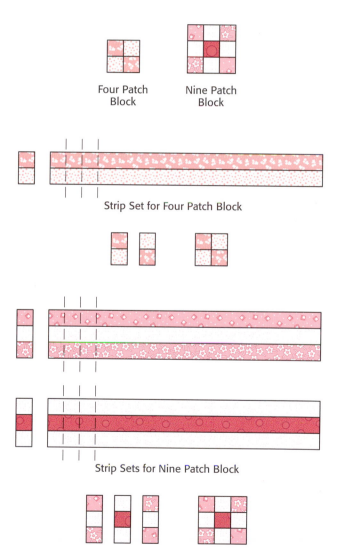

Four Patch Block   Nine Patch Block

Strip Set for Four Patch Block

Strip Sets for Nine Patch Block

HALF-SQUARE TRIANGLE UNITS

Several of the quilts in this book contain half-square triangle units, also called triangle squares. See "Sunny Sailors" on page 74. I make these units the easy way, without cutting triangles. I also cut the squares slightly oversized to make the math easy and to enable you to trim and square up the blocks after piecing.

"Sunny Sailors" Block

1. Cut the square 1" larger than the desired finished size of the half-square triangle unit. The size to cut is given in the quilt cutting directions.

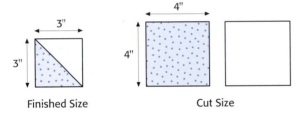

Finished Size   Cut Size

2. Layer the squares right sides together in pairs with the lighter color on top of the darker color.

3. Using a pencil and a rotary-cutting ruler, draw a diagonal line from corner to corner on the wrong side of the lighter fabric. Sew ¼" away from the drawn line on each side.

4. Cut on the drawn line with a rotary cutter and ruler.

5. Flip open the triangles, press the seam allowance toward the darker color, and trim away the little triangles or "dog ears" that extend beyond the block at the corners. Trim and square up the block to the desired unfinished size. Each pair of squares will yield two half-square triangle units.

HOURGLASS TRIANGLE UNITS

The following little trick with a half-square triangle is so clever, I'm reluctant to mention it to non-quilters because they'll find out we are not as brilliant as they thought. The "Little Buddy" quilt on page 56 features the Hourglass block.

1. Follow the steps in the preceding section for making half-square triangle units.

2. Cut across the sewn half-square units on the diagonal to make two triangle units.

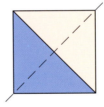 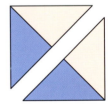

3. Arrange the triangles as shown and stitch the Hourglass blocks.

FOLDED CORNERS

One of the most satisfying tricks quiltmakers have at their disposal is what I call folded corners. It's another way of piecing triangles without actually cutting triangles and sewing on the bias. All you do is cut squares and stitch them to the corner of another patch, usually a square or a rectangle. Many of the quilts in this book feature blocks created with this technique.

1. Cut squares the size given in the quilt directions. Draw a diagonal line from corner to corner on the back of the squares.

Mary's Helpful Hint

I like to stack up the squares and sit and draw a faint diagonal pencil line on each square while I watch a good video or a baseball game. As I finish each square I position it on the larger square or rectangle, ready to stitch on the machine.

2. Position the squares on the pieces called for in the quilt directions, and sew on the drawn line.

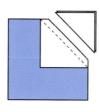

3. Cut ¼" from the seam line. Flip open the triangle and press the seam allowance toward the darker color.

Trim.   Press.

APPLIQUÉ PRIMER

APPLIQUÉ INVOLVES TURNING UNDER the edges of shapes and sewing them to a larger piece of fabric. Resourceful quilters have developed many clever methods to accomplish this time-honored quiltmaking technique. The methods that follow are my favorites for the simple shapes used in this book.

Face-and-Turn Appliqué

1. Make a template of your appliqué shape using a stiff paper (an index card or a greeting card). Do not add a seam allowance.

2. With right sides together, layer your appliqué fabric with a piece of lightweight cotton or featherweight sew-in interfacing and pin the layers together.

3. Using a blue water-soluble marking pen, trace the desired number of shapes onto the interfacing, leaving a ½" space between the shapes for a seam allowance.

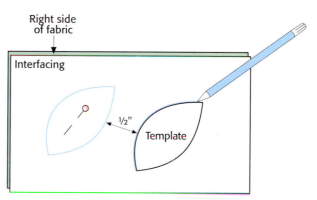

4. Using a very short stitch length, carefully machine stitch on the marked line around all of the shapes.

5. Cut out all the shapes, leaving a scant ⅛" seam allowance.

6. Using a spray bottle, spray the pieces with water to remove the marked lines.

7. Making a slit as big as necessary in the backing fabric or interfacing of each piece, turn the appliqué shapes right side out and gently smooth the points and curves using a knitting needle or chopstick. Press. (*Note:* The dampness from the spray seems to make it easier to push out the curves and points.)

8. Since you have enclosed the unfinished edges of your appliqué pieces, you can simply bar-tack them onto your quilt using a matching thread, or you can use the hand or machine appliqué methods described in the following sections.

Paper Template Appliqué

1. Make a template of your appliqué shape using a stiff paper (an index card or greeting card). Do not add a seam allowance. Trace the template and cut out a paper template for each appliqué shape.

2. Pin a paper template to the back of the appliqué fabric.

3. Cut out the fabric adding approximately ¼" seam allowance.

4. Using your thumb and index finger, fold a hem over the edge of the paper template and baste the folded fabric to the template.

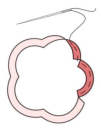

5. Pin or baste the shapes in position on the background fabric and appliqué by hand as instructed in the next section, "Hand Stitch Appliqué."

6. Remove the basting stitches, carefully cut a slit in the background fabric behind the appliqué, and remove the paper template.

Hand Stitch Appliqué

1. Using a single thread that matches the appliqué fabric, insert the needle from the back of your background fabric, up and through the fold of your appliqué piece, catching one or two threads.

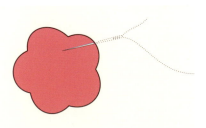

2. Insert the needle back down at the same spot but through only the background fabric. Bring the needle up again, about ⅛" from the previous stitch and through both layers as before.

3. To end your stitching, take a few tiny backstitches on the back of your work behind the appliqué.

4. After you have completed stitching, remove any basting stitches. Cut a slit in the background fabric to remove the paper template if you used one.

Invisible Zigzag Stitch Appliqué

This technique is a simple alternative to hand appliqué and gives surprisingly good results. The key to the success of this method is the use of fine, high-quality 100% cotton thread with a silk finish. Sew each appliqué piece with its own color of thread. Use an open-toe embroidery foot on your machine for better visibility. Because I use the face-and-turn method of preparing my appliqué shapes, I do not need to use a stabilizer. If you find that your stitches create puckers, use a tear-away stabilizer under the fabric when doing machine appliqué.

1. Machine baste your appliqué shapes in place.

2. Set your zigzag to a 1 mm stitch length and width. Slowly stitch around the appliqué shape so that the needle takes one stitch in the appliqué piece and one stitch in the background fabric. For points and curves, position the needle in the down position, raise your presser foot and pivot as needed. Zigzag around the appliqué shape, stitching over the first few stitches at the beginning to secure the threads.

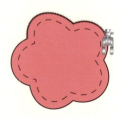

3. After you have completed stitching, remove the machine basting.

Fusible Appliqué

HeatnBond, Wonder-Under, and Steam-A-Seam are brand names of some of the fusible webs available for the quick and easy fusible appliqué technique. You do not have to hem the edges of the shapes, because the glue will prevent the edges from fraying.

1. Using a template and a pencil, draw the shapes onto the paper side of the fusible web. Note that the finished appliqué will be the reverse of the traced shape.

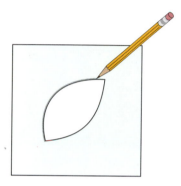

2. Following the manufacturer's instructions, iron the paper to the wrong side of the fabric.

3. Cut out the shapes on the drawn lines.

4. Peel away the paper and position the shapes on the background fabric.

5. Iron the shapes to the background fabric.

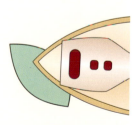

6. If you like, you can topstitch the shapes with contrasting thread using a straight, zigzag, or buttonhole stitch.

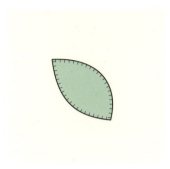

Mary's Helpful Hint

If you plan to do a hand buttonhole stitch around your fused appliqué shapes, be sure to use a lightweight fusible web. Heavyweight fusible products are difficult to stitch through.

SQUARING UP THE BLOCKS

ONCE YOU HAVE COMPLETED THE BLOCKS for your quilt, it is time to measure them. If they are within $\frac{1}{16}$" of each other you can skip squaring up the blocks.

1. Measure all the blocks for your quilt. Determine the size of the smallest block and trim the other blocks to that size. For example, if your blocks should be 6½" and you notice that some of them are 6⅜" or even 6¼", you will need to trim all of them to 6¼". If you trim a small amount from all 4 sides of each block, the blocks will be even and easy to assemble into the quilt top. Keep in mind that if you reduce the size of your blocks, you may also have to stitch them with less than a ¼" seam. You must also reduce the size of any sashings or setting blocks if they are a part of your quilt.

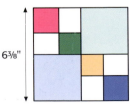

6⅜"

2. Use a rotary cutter and a square ruler to trim the blocks. Place two pieces of masking tape on the ruler; in this example, place the tape on the 6¼" lines of the ruler. Mark the ruler with a dot of tape in the center of the block size. In this example, half of 6¼" would be 3⅛"; therefore, 3⅛" would be the center of your block. Insert a small pin in the block to mark the center.

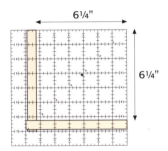

6¼"

6¼"

3. Align the center of the ruler with the center of the block and trim $\frac{1}{16}$" from each side of the blocks.

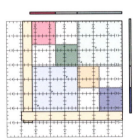

4. Rotate the block, line up the ruler, and trim the other two sides of the block. This will take only a few minutes and save you many moments of frustration.

ASSEMBLING THE QUILT TOP

WHEN YOU HAVE MADE ALL THE BLOCKS and cut the sashing or setting pieces as needed, you are ready to assemble the quilt top.

Quilts with Blocks Set Side by Side

1. Arrange the blocks following the illustration provided with each quilt. Rotate or alternate the blocks as needed so that the pressed seams of the blocks will butt up against each other for easier matching.

2. Join the blocks in horizontal or vertical rows as shown for the quilt.

3. Press the seams in opposite directions from row to row, or press toward alternate blocks from row to row so the seams will butt together when the rows are joined.

4. Join the rows, making sure to match the seams and points between the blocks.

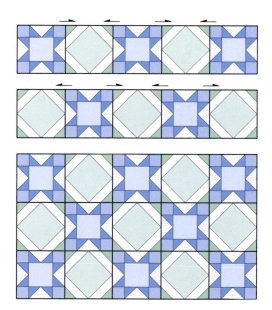

Quilts with Sashing Strips and Cornerstones

For quilts with sashing strips, follow the illustrations for your project to arrange the blocks and sashing strips. Join the blocks and vertical sashing strips in rows. Press the seams toward the sashing strips. Join the rows of blocks and horizontal sashing strips.

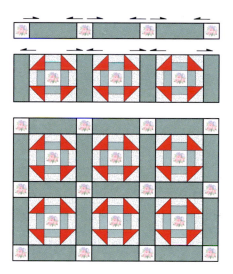

Quilts Set on Point

For quilts set on point, arrange the blocks, setting blocks, and corner and side triangles as shown in the diagram for the quilt you are making. Pay close attention to the placement of the corner and side triangles. Join the diagonal rows of blocks and triangles to create the quilt top.

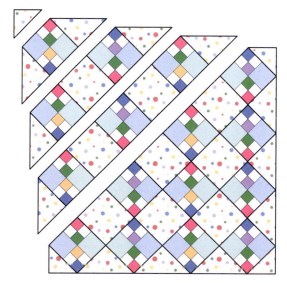

Borders

Borders should always be cut to fit the center measurements of the quilt. If you cut them without measuring the quilt through the center, the borders might not fit properly and your quilts will end up looking wavy or puckered. Normal stretching during construction often leaves the side edges of the quilt a little longer than the center. Sometimes each edge of a quilt is a different measurement. So measure the quilt through the center and cut the borders to fit that length. For the projects in this book, always stitch the side borders first and then the top and bottom.

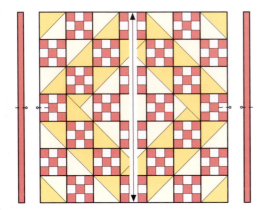

Measure top to bottom through the center.
Mark centers.

Mary's Helpful Hint

When I make baby quilts, I usually include an inner border in a strong color that finishes at 1" wide. This accents the quilt center and visually separates it. For the outer borders, I choose a medium color to act as the final frame around the quilt. For most quilts, these are 3" wide finished.

INNER BORDERS

To attach inner borders, follow these steps.

1. Measure the length of the quilt through the middle as shown.

2. Cut 2 strips that measurement.

3. Mark the center of the borders and the center of the sides of the quilt top as shown.

4. Pin the inner borders to the quilt top, matching the ends and centers and easing as necessary.

5. Stitch the inner side borders to the quilt top. Press the seams toward the borders.

6. Measure the width of the quilt through the center including the side borders.

7. Cut 2 strips that measurement.

8. Mark and pin the borders as you did in steps 3 and 4, and stitch the inner borders to the top and bottom of the quilt. Press toward the borders.

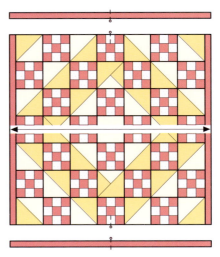

Measure side to side through the center.
Mark centers.

OUTER BORDERS

Measure the length of the quilt through the center including the inner borders. Cut and attach the outer borders following the same steps as for the inner borders in the preceding section.

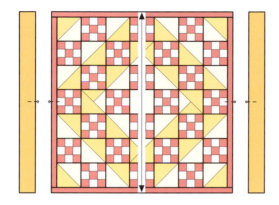

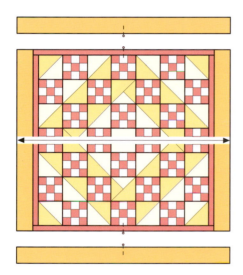

BORDERS WITH CORNERSTONES

Some of the quilts in this book ("Playmates," "Pipsqueak Picnic," and "Bright Garden") include squares or pieced blocks in the corners of their outer borders. These are called cornerstones. Follow these steps to attach borders with cornerstones.

1. Measure the length and width of the quilt through the center.

2. Cut the four border strips to those measurements.

3. Stitch the side borders to the quilt. Press toward the borders.

4. Sew the corner blocks to the top and bottom border strips.

5. Stitch the top and bottom borders to the quilt. Press toward the borders.

PREPARING TO QUILT

YOUR QUILT TOP IS NOW COMPLETE and you need to decide how you will quilt it. If the design needs to be marked on the quilt, marking should be done before layering the quilt with the backing and batting.

Backing

Take some time when selecting the backing of your baby quilt; people will see it more than they would with an ordinary quilt. The back of most baby quilts can be made from a single piece of interesting or pretty fabric. Of course, you can use up scraps and strips left over from the blocks to make the backing fun, or funny, or pretty, depending on the quilt. You can keep it simple with a single fabric or you can be as creative with the back of the quilt as you are with the front. Just be sure the fabric on the back does not show through the lightest areas on the front, causing them to look dingy.

The backing should be cut 4" to 6" larger than the quilt top. Some of the quilts are wider than 42", so they will need to have pieced backs. You can place the seams anywhere you want. The following diagrams show two possible arrangements.

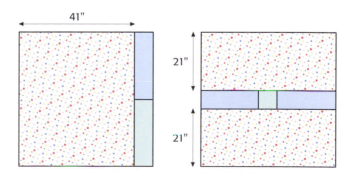

Layering and Basting

Press the backing fabric and quilt top. Open and unroll the batting and allow it to "relax" overnight. Spread the backing wrong side up on a clean, flat surface. Use masking tape to anchor the backing to the surface without stretching the fabric. Spread the quilt batting on the backing, making sure it covers the entire backing and is smooth. Center the pressed and marked top on the batting and backing, right side up. Align borders and straight lines of the quilt top with the edges of the backing. Pin the layers together along the edge with large straight pins to hold the layers smooth.

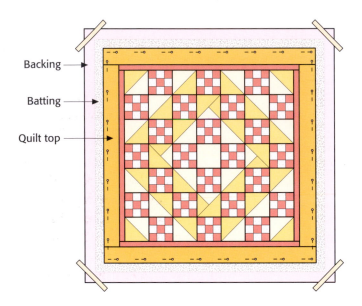

If you will be machine quilting your quilt, see the following section "Safety-Pin Basting for Machine Quilting." If you will be hand quilting, see "Hand Basting" at right.

SAFETY- PIN BASTING FOR MACHINE QUILTING

Machine quilters use one-inch safety pins for basting a quilt. This is because thread basting catches in the presser foot of the sewing machine.

1. Layer the backing, batting, and quilt top as shown. Start pinning in the center and work toward the outer edges of the quilt, spacing the pins about 4" to 6" apart. Insert the pins as you would straight pins; do not close them yet. Avoid pinning over

design lines and seam lines where you intend to stitch in the ditch.

2. After pinning, use a needle and thread to baste a line of stitches around the outside edges. This will keep the edges from raveling while you quilt and will also keep the edges aligned when you stitch the binding to the quilt.

3. Remove the layered quilt from the hard surface, check the back to be sure it is smooth, and close the safety pins.

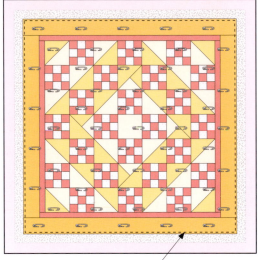

Hand baste around outer edge.

HAND BASTING

When hand quilting, hand baste the three layers together with thread; safety pins would get in the way of hoops or frames. Use a long needle and light-colored thread. If you thread your needle without cutting the thread off the spool, you will be able to baste at least two rows without rethreading your needle.

1. Starting at the center of the quilt, use long running stitches to baste across the quilt from side to side and top to bottom.

2. Continue basting, creating a grid of parallel lines 6" to 8" apart. Complete the basting with a line of careful stitches around the outside edges. This will keep the edges from raveling while you quilt and

will also keep the edges aligned when you stitch the binding to the quilt. After the basting is complete, remove the pins and masking tape.

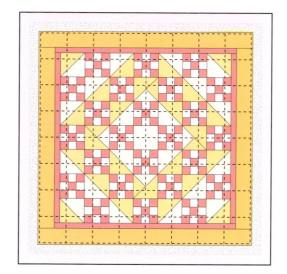

MACHINE QUILTING

Use a fine, 100% cotton silk-finish thread. Thread your bobbin with the same quality thread. Look for a machine needle with a large eye. This will keep the thread from fraying or shredding.

Walking Foot

Many machines have a walking foot or even-feed foot either built into the machine or as an attachment. This foot works on top of the fabric to move the top layer at the same speed as the bottom layer. This moves the quilt layers through the sewing machine evenly to help prevent puckering. Use this type of foot for straight lines, grid quilting, and large, simple curves.

Walking Foot   Straight-Line Quilting

Darning Foot

Use a darning foot for curved designs and stipple quilting. This allows free movement of the fabric under the foot of your sewing machine. This is called free-motion quilting and, with practice, it enables you to produce beautiful designs quickly. Choose designs that have continuous lines and that don't require a lot of starting and stopping.

Darning Foot   Free-Motion Quilting

1. Lower the feed dogs on your machine when quilting with a darning foot. This allows you to guide the fabric under the needle as if the needle were a stationary pencil.

2. The stitch length is determined by the speed with which you run the machine and how much you move the fabric under the needle. This is a bit like "walking and chewing gum at the same time," but you will get used to it with a little practice. The effort is well worth it, because you can complete a baby quilt in a single evening.

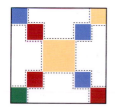

MACHINE QUILTING

I usually pay a professional to machine quilt my baby quilts. In the last few years, machine quilting has become a beautiful art form in its own right. It has also developed into an excellent cottage industry for many women. While machine quilting is faster than hand quilting, it is still an art that requires creativity and skill. Practice will make it fun and easy.

1. Plan a quilting design that has continuous long, straight lines and gentle curves.

2. Use a sewing machine needle with a larger eye, such as size 90/14, that will not shred the thread.

3. Experiment with different threads to find one you like. Many machine quilters prefer silk-finish cotton thread.

4. Keep the spacing between quilting lines consistent over the entire quilt.

5. Make sure to adjust your chair to a comfortable height.

6. Practice with layers of fabric and scrap batting until you get the feel of controlling the motion of the fabric with your hands. Running the machine fairly fast enables you to sew smoother lines of quilting.

7. To start and stop, shorten the stitch length for the first and last ⅛" to ¼".

8. Practice stitching some scribbles, zigzags, and curves. Try a heart or a star. Be patient. You can go faster on the machine but it does require some skill and practice.

9. Roll your layered quilt up like a scroll. Starting in the center and using the walking foot, stitch all the lines from top to bottom. Always start at the same end so that the rows won't pull in opposite directions. Re-roll your quilt from the sides and repeat stitching the straight lines in that direction. Next repeat with the diagonal lines. Remove the pins as you get the areas secured. Remember to take several breaks and stretch your back.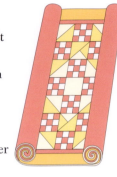

10. When you have completed all the straight-line quilting, switch to your darning foot, lower the feed dog, and start the free-motion quilting. Stipple quilting in the background areas gives a lovely texture and doesn't require any prior marking. Pretend that you are drawing jigsaw puzzle lines on your quilt—lots of curvy lines without any loops. Try to end up at an intersection where you can "jump" across to the next area to be stitched.

HAND QUILTING

AN HEIRLOOM QUILT FOR A very special little one deserves hand quilting. For some quilters, the most enjoyable part of making a quilt is the hand quilting. It is relaxing to sit and stitch, while visiting with friends or riding in the car. Quilting is simply a short running stitch that goes through all three layers of the quilt.

Hand quilt in a frame, in a hoop, on a tabletop, or on your lap. Use a thick thread designed for hand quilting. Quilting thread is less likely to tangle than regular sewing thread. Use a short sturdy needle (called a Between) in a size 7 or 8. As you become more experienced with hand quilting, switch to a smaller needle (a higher number). A smaller needle will enable you to take smaller stitches. Use a thimble with a rim around the top edge to help push the needle through the layers.

1. Cut the thread 24" long, thread the needle, and tie a small knot. Starting about 1" from where you want the quilting to begin, insert the needle through the top and batting only. Bring the needle up where the quilting will start. Gently tug on the knot until it pops through the quilt top and catches in the batting.

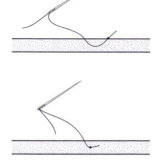

Tug on the thread until the knot goes between the layers.

2. Insert the needle and push it straight down through all the layers using the middle finger with the thimble. Then rock the needle up and down through all layers, "loading" three or four stitches on the needle. Place your other hand under the quilt to make sure the needle has penetrated all three layers with each stitch.

3. Pull the needle through, aiming toward yourself as you work. Continue in this way, taking small, even stitches through all three layers.

4. To end a line of quilting, make a small knot close to the quilt top and then insert the needle through the top and batting only, bringing it up about ½" away. Pop the knot through the fabric into the batting. Clip the thread near the surface of the quilt.

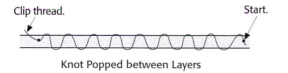

Clip thread.   Start.

Knot Popped between Layers

FINISHING AND BINDING

When all the quilting is completed, remove any stray pins and basting thread, but leave the basting stitches around the edges. Trim the batting and backing even with the quilt top. Make sure the corners are square. What a wonderful moment this is!

Making a Hanging Sleeve

If you are going to hang the quilt, attach a hanging sleeve or rod pocket to the back before you bind it.

1. From the leftover backing fabric cut a piece the width of your quilt by 8". On each end, fold over a ½" hem and then fold under again; press and stitch.

2. Place the long edges wrong sides together and stitch the sleeve into a tube. Press and baste to the top of the back of the quilt. When you machine stitch the binding into place you will also stitch the sleeve to the top, hiding the raw edges in the binding.

Quilt back

Binding Your Quilt

Start by cutting binding strips. I like to make double-fold bias binding because this technique wears well and creates a smooth appearance. However, if you have a striped fabric or other fabric with a directional design, cutting on the straight grain might give you the look you want.

1. To make bias binding strips, use the 45-degree angle line on your large cutting ruler as a guide. Cut enough strips to go comfortably around the

quilt with about 12" extra for mitering corners and lapping the ends. Cut the strips 2¼" wide.

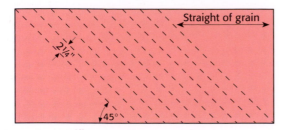

2. Join the binding strips with a diagonal seam. Fold and press the binding wrong sides together.

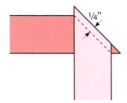

3. Leaving the first 10" unsewn, stitch the binding using a ¼" seam allowance.

4. Stop stitching ¼" from the corner of the quilt and backstitch.

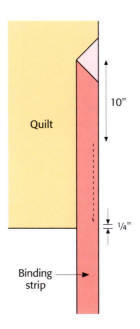

5. Remove the quilt from the sewing machine. Fold the binding at a 45-degree angle up away from the quilt. Then fold it back down so that it is even with the next side as shown.

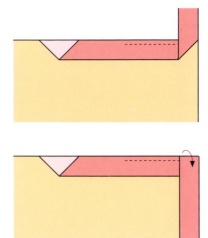

6. Using a ¼" seam allowance, continue stitching along the next side.

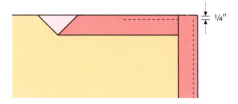

7. Continue stitching in this manner around all four sides, catching the sleeve on the top edge. Stop stitching 10" from where you started.

8. Remove the quilt from the machine and lay it on a flat surface. Fold the unsewn binding ends back on themselves so they just meet in the middle. Pin or press both strips to mark this junction.

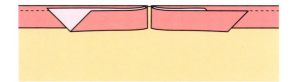

9. Unfold both ends of the binding and mark the centers where the crease lines intersect. With right sides together, overlap the ends of the binding at right angles, matching the crease lines and marks in the middle. Pin and sew across the intersection at a 45° angle. Trim the excess fabric and press the seam open.

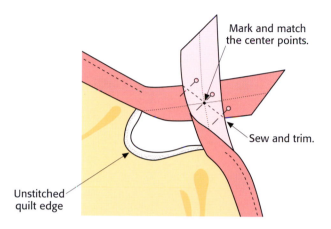

Mark and match the center points.

Sew and trim.

Unstitched quilt edge

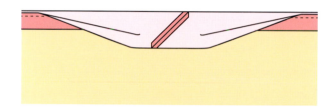

10. Finish stitching the binding to the quilt edge.

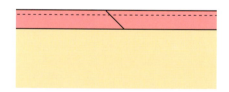

11. Fold the binding around to the back of the quilt and blind stitch it down, using your machine stitching line as a guide. A miter will form at each corner. Fold the corners in place and stitch.

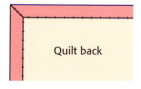

Quilt back

Adding a Quilt Label

Labeling your quilt is an important finishing touch. A label can be as simple or as elaborate as you wish. Use a plain fabric that coordinates with your backing fabric and include the name of the quilt, your name, your city and state, the date, the name of the baby who is the recipient if it is a gift, and any other interesting or important information. This can be embroidered or written with a permanent pen. If you are using a pen, iron freezer paper to the back of the fabric to stabilize the fabric while writing.

Family Hearts
for Audrey Hickey
made by
Mary Hickey
Silverdale, Washington
2003

COBBLESTONES

Simplicity itself, blue and yellow squares give us the feeling of an artist's color study in this uncomplicated quilt. It's so easy, you can make it almost as fast as you can read the instructions. Look for three shades of blue and an exuberant yellow. (Just four fabrics!) Place the yellow in all the blue blocks and one of the blues in the yellow blocks. Think of the lightest blue and the yellow as lights and then just alternate the lights and darks. Or, make the quilt with pink and green or purple and aqua. Whimsical machine quilting of loopy curves and stars adds to the quilt's simple charm.

Materials

All yardages are based on 42"-wide fabric.

¾ yd. medium blue for blocks and outer border

⅝ yd. yellow for blocks and inner border

¼ yd. dark blue for blocks

¼ yd. light blue for blocks

1⅜ yds. fabric for backing

⅜ yd. fabric for binding

35" x 39" batting

Making the Blocks

1. Sew a dark blue strip to opposite sides of a 2" yellow strip. Press toward the blue fabric. Cut the strip set into a total of 8 segments, each 2" wide.

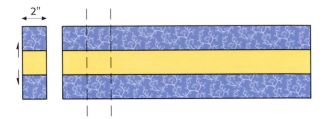

Cutting

Fabric	Used For	Number to Cut	Size to Cut	Second Cut
Dark blue	Blocks (8)	3 strips	2" x 42"	Cut strips in half to make a total of 6 strips, 2" x 21".
Yellow	Blocks (7)	5 strips	2" x 42"	Cut strips in half to make a total of 10 strips, 2" x 21". (You will use 9.)
	Inner borders*	4 strips	1½" x 42"	2 strips, 1½" x 27½" 2 strips, 1½" x 25"
Medium blue	Blocks (7)	4 strips	2" x 42"	Cut strips in half to make a total of 8 strips, 2" x 21". (You will use 7.)
	Outer borders*	4 strips	3½" x 42"	2 strips, 3½" x 29½" 2 strips, 3½" x 31"
Light blue	Blocks (8)	3 strips	2" x 42"	Cut strips in half to make a total of 6 strips, 2" x 21".

* Wait until you have completed the center of the quilt before making the second cut for borders. Measure the quilt through the center and cut the border strips to fit that measurement.

QUILT SIZE: 30½" x 35" • BLOCK SIZE: 4½"

Designed and pieced by Mary Hickey. Quilted by Dawn Kelly.

2. Place the 8 segments on 2 strips of the dark blue and stitch them together as shown. Cut the pieced units apart. Press toward the blue fabric.

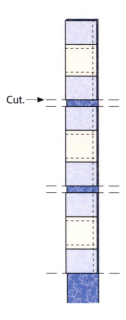

Cut. ➞

3. Place the segments on 2 more strips of the dark blue and stitch 8 blocks. Cut the blocks apart as shown. Press toward the blue fabric.

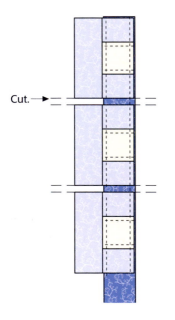

Cut. ➞

4. Sew a 2" medium blue strip to opposite sides of a 2" yellow strip. Press toward the blue fabric. Cut the strip set into a total of 7 segments, each 2" wide.

5. Place the segments on 2 strips of the medium blue and stitch them together as you did in step 2. Cut apart. Press toward the blue fabric.

6. Place the segments on 2 additional strips of the medium blue and stitch 7 blocks. Cut the blocks apart as in step 3. Press toward the blue fabric.

7. Sew a light blue strip to opposite sides of a 2" yellow strip. Press toward the blue fabric. Cut the strip set into a total of 8 segments, each 2" wide.

8. Place the segments on 2 strips of the light blue and stitch them together as you did in step 2. Cut apart. Press toward the blue fabric.

9. Place the segments on 2 additional strips of the light blue and stitch 8 blocks. Cut the blocks apart as in step 3. Press toward the blue fabric.

10. Sew a 2" yellow strip to opposite sides of a medium blue strip. Press toward the blue fabric. Cut the strip set into a total of 7 segments, each 2" wide.

11. Place the segments on 2 strips of the yellow and stitch them together as you did in step 2. Cut apart. Press toward the blue fabric.

12. Place the segments on 2 additional strips of the yellow and stitch 7 blocks. Cut the blocks apart as in step 3.

Assembling the Quilt

1. Arrange the blocks in 6 rows of 5 blocks each, alternating the light and dark blocks.

2. Sew the blocks together in rows, pressing the seams toward the dark and medium blue blocks.

3. Sew the rows together, pressing the seams all in one direction.

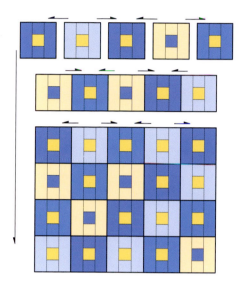

Adding the Borders

Refer to "Borders" on pages 18–19 for more details, if needed. Measure the quilt through the center and cut the border strips to fit that measurement.

1. Sew the inner borders to the sides of the quilt. Press toward the border.

2. Sew the inner borders to the top and bottom of the quilt. Press.

3. Repeat with the outer borders, pressing toward the outer border.

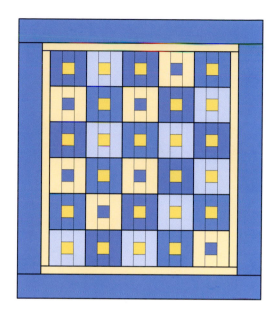

Finishing the Quilt

Refer to the general directions, beginning with "Preparing to Quilt" on page 19, for more details on quilting and finishing.

1. Cut the backing fabric so it is approximately 4" to 6" larger than the quilt top.

2. Layer the backing, batting, and quilt top, and baste the layers together.

3. Hand or machine quilt as desired. The quilt shown was machine quilted with lighthearted loops, curves, and stars in both the blocks and the borders.

4. Trim the batting and backing fabric so the edges are even with the quilt-top edges, and bind the quilt. Add a hanging sleeve, if desired, and a label.

PINK LEMONADE

Classic strawberry-colored Nine Patch blocks pair with luscious lemon yellows in this classic, simple quilt. The Nine Patch block is much beloved by quilters. It is direct, straightforward, and always makes an adorable quilt. Alternating the pink Nine Patch blocks with yellow and white triangle blocks creates an interesting, yet very easy, quilt. You can see that I have arranged the colors of the triangle blocks to make a diamond shape around the perky pink Nine Patch blocks. This adds interest and depth to the quilt without adding difficulty.

Materials

All yardages are based on 42"-wide fabric unless otherwise stated.

⅝ yd. yellow for triangle blocks

½ yd. pinkish-white for Nine Patch blocks

½ yd. yellowish-white for triangle blocks

½ yd. dark yellow for outer border

¼ yd. or scraps of 5 pinks for Nine Patch blocks

¼ yd. each or scraps of 5 different pinks for Nine Patch blocks and inner border (for a total of about ¾ yd.)

1⅝ yds. fabric for backing

⅜ yd. fabric for binding

43" x 43" batting

Making the Nine Patch Blocks

1. Sew a 2" pink strip to opposite sides of a pinkish-white strip. Press seams toward the darker fabric. Make 3 strip sets. Cut the strip sets into a total of 48 segments, each 2" wide.

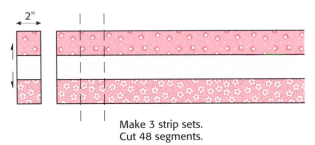

Make 3 strip sets.
Cut 48 segments.

Cutting

Fabric	Used For	Number to Cut	Size to Cut	Second Cut
Pinks	Nine Patch blocks	8 strips	2" x 42"	–
	Inner border*	4 strips	1½" x 42"	2 strips, 1½" x 32"
				2 strips, 1½" x 34"
Pinkish-white	Nine Patch blocks	7 strips	2" x 42"	–
Yellow	Triangle blocks	2 strips	5½" x 42"	10 squares, 5½" x 5½"
		3 squares	5¾" x 5¾"	–
Yellowish-white	Triangle blocks	2 strips	5½" x 42"	10 squares, 5½" x 5½"
		1 square	5" x 5"	–
		1 square	5¾" x 5¾""	–
Dark yellow	Outer border*	4 strips	3½" x 42"	2 strips, 3½" x 34"
				2 strips, 3½" x 40"

* Wait until you have completed the center of the quilt before making the second cut for borders. Measure the quilt through the center and cut the border strips to fit that measurement.

QUILT SIZE: 39½" x 39½" • BLOCK SIZE: 4½"

Designed and pieced by Mary Hickey. Quilted by Fannie Schwartz.

2. Sew a pinkish-white strip to opposite sides of a 2" pink strip. Press toward the darker fabric. Make 2 strip sets. Cut the strip sets into a total of 24 segments, each 2" wide.

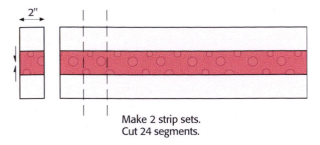

Make 2 strip sets.
Cut 24 segments.

3. Arrange the segments in groups to create the Nine Patch blocks as shown. Stitch 24 blocks.

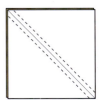

Make 24.

Making the Triangle Blocks

1. Layer the yellow and yellowish-white 5½" squares in pairs, right sides together, with the lighter color on top. Using a pencil and your rotary-cutting ruler, draw a diagonal line through the center of each yellowish-white square. Draw another line ¼" away on both sides of the first line. Stitch on the second and third drawn lines.

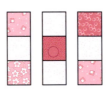

2. Cut along the center line, flip open the squares, and press toward the darker fabric. Measure and trim to 5" x 5". Make 20 triangle squares.

 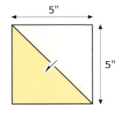

Make 20.

3. Layer 2 yellow 5¾" squares and cut them once on the diagonal. Set these triangles aside.

4. Layer the remaining yellow 5¾" square and the yellowish-white 5¾" square, right sides together, with the lighter color on top. Using a pencil and your rotary-cutting ruler, draw a diagonal line through the center of the yellowish-white square. Draw another line ¼" away on both sides of the first line. Stitch on the second and third drawn lines.

5. Cut along the center line, flip open the squares, and press toward the darker fabric.

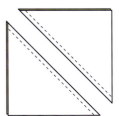 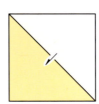

6. Cut the sewn squares once on the diagonal as shown.

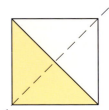 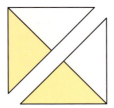

7. Assemble the triangles from step 3 and the units from step 6 to make 4 blocks as shown. Trim to 5" x 5".

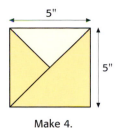

Make 4.

Assembling the Quilt

1. Arrange the blocks in 7 rows of 7 blocks each, alternating the blocks and orienting the setting blocks as shown in the quilt assembly diagram.

2. Sew the Nine Patch and setting blocks together in rows, pressing the seams toward the setting blocks.

3. Sew the rows together, pressing the seams all in one direction.

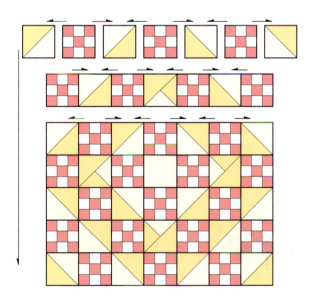

Adding the Borders

Refer to "Borders" on pages 18–19 for more details, if needed. Measure the quilt through the center and cut the border strips to fit that measurement.

1. Sew the inner borders to the sides of the quilt. Press toward the border.

2. Sew the inner borders to the top and bottom of the quilt. Press.

3. Repeat with the outer borders, pressing toward the outer border.

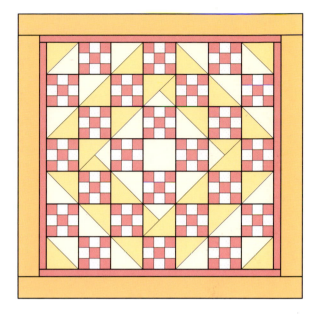

Finishing the Quilt

Refer to the general directions, beginning with "Preparing to Quilt" on page 19, for more details on quilting and finishing.

1. Cut the backing fabric so it is approximately 4" to 6" larger than the quilt top.

2. Layer the backing, batting, and quilt top, and baste the layers together.

3. Hand or machine quilt as desired. The quilt shown was hand quilted with a moon and star in the yellow blocks, in-the-ditch quilting in the Nine Patch blocks, and a simple cable in the borders.

4. Trim the batting and backing even with the quilt-top edges, and bind the quilt. Add a hanging sleeve, if desired, and a label.

WONDER BABY

Double four-patch units are so easy, they just zoom together and make a wonderful, complex-looking quilt in no time. Everyone will think you are a quilting genius. Polka dots are especially fun. This one reminds me of Wonder Bread packaging. You'll enjoy making this simple quilt as much as the baby will enjoy using it.

Materials

All yardages are based on 42"-wide fabric unless otherwise stated.

1⅛ yds. polka dot fabric for setting squares and outer border

⅜ yd. white print for block backgrounds

⅜ yd. blue print for blocks and inner border

¼ yd. pale blue for blocks

¼ yd. pale green for blocks

⅛ yd. green for blocks

⅛ yd. pink for blocks

⅛ yd. or fat quarter purple for blocks

⅛ yd. or fat quarter yellow for blocks

1½ yds. fabric for backing

⅜ yd. fabric for binding

40" x 40" batting

Cutting

Fabric	Used For	Number to Cut	Size to Cut	Second Cut
White print	Blocks	4 strips	1¾" x 42"	Cut 1 strip in half.
Pink	Blocks	1 strip	1¾" x 42"	–
Blue	Blocks	1 strip	1¾" x 42"	–
	Inner border*	4 strips	1½" x 42"	2 strips, 1½" x 28" 2 strips, 1½" x 31"
Green	Blocks	1 strip	1¾" x 42"	–
Yellow	Blocks	1 strip	1¾" x 21"	–
Purple	Blocks	1 strip	1¾" x 21"	–
Pale blue	Blocks	2 strips	3" x 42"	16 squares, 3" x 3"
Pale green	Blocks	2 strips	3" x 42"	16 squares, 3" x 3"
Polka dot	Setting squares	2 strips	5½" x 42"	9 squares, 5½" x 5½"
	Corner triangles	Use remainder of 5½" strip from setting squares to cut 2 squares.	4¾" x 4¾"	Cut once on the diagonal to make 4 corner triangles.
	Side triangles	3 squares	8½" x 8½"	Cut twice on the diagonal to make 12 side triangles.
	Outer border*	4 strips	3½" x 42"	2 strips, 3½" x 31" 2 strips, 3½" x 37½"

* Wait until you have completed the center of the quilt before making the second cut for borders. Measure the quilt through the center and cut the border strips to fit that measurement.

QUILT SIZE: 36" x 36" • BLOCK SIZE: 5"

Designed and pieced by Mary Hickey. Quilted by Dawn Kelly.

Note from Mary

Polka dot fabrics are a perfect starting point for a baby quilt. I love working with them because they are playful and cheerful. Look for a fabric with several colors of dots and then gather fabrics that echo the dot colors. Each block in this quilt has a pink, a blue, and a green square. Notice that half of the blocks have a yellow square and half have a purple square.

Making the Blocks

1. Sew a 1¾" x 42" white strip to each of the pink, blue, and green 1¾" x 42" strips to make 3 strip sets as shown. Cut each of the strip sets into 16 segments, 1¾" wide.

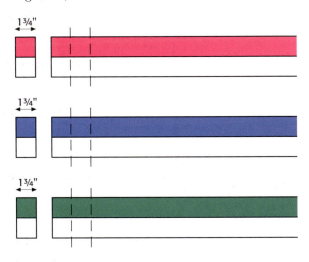

2. Make 16 pink-and-green four-patch units.

Make 16.

3. Sew one of the 1¾" x 21" white print strips to the yellow strip and sew the other to the purple strip. Cut each of the strip sets into 8 segments, 1¾" wide, as shown.

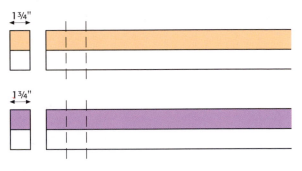

4. Join these segments with the remaining segments from step 1 to make 8 blue-and-yellow four-patch units and 8 blue-and-purple four-patch units.

Make 8.　　　Make 8.

5. Sew the pink-and-green four-patch units to the pale blue squares, orienting your four-patch units as shown. Repeat to sew the 8 blue-and-yellow units and the 8 blue-and-purple units to the pale green squares, orienting the four-patch units as shown. Press seam allowances toward the light-colored squares.

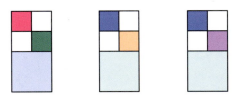

6. Arrange the four-patch units, pairing them as shown. Sew the pieces together to make 16 blocks.

Assembling the Quilt

1. Arrange the blocks, setting squares, corner triangles, and side triangles in diagonal rows.

2. Sew the blocks together in diagonal rows, pressing the seams toward the setting squares.

3. Sew the rows together; press the seams all in one direction.

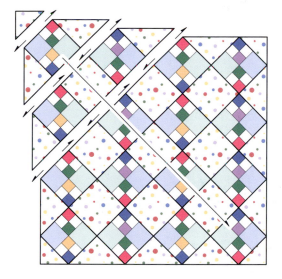

Adding the Borders

Refer to "Borders" on pages 18–19 for more details, if needed. Measure the quilt through the center and cut the border strips to fit that measurement.

1. Sew the inner borders to the sides of the quilt. Press toward the border.

2. Sew the inner borders to the top and bottom of the quilt. Press.

3. Repeat with the outer borders, pressing toward the outer border.

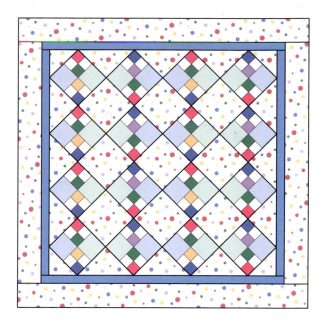

Finishing the Quilt

Refer to the general directions, beginning with "Preparing to Quilt" on page 19, for more details on quilting and finishing.

1. Cut the backing fabric so it is approximately 4" to 6" larger than the quilt top.

2. Layer the backing, batting, and quilt top, and baste the layers together.

3. Hand or machine quilt as desired. The quilt shown was machine quilted with four petals in each four-patch unit, circles around the blocks, and a looping design in the border.

4. Trim the batting and backing fabric so the edges are even with the quilt-top edges, and bind the quilt. Add a hanging sleeve, if desired, and a label.

Baby Buckaroos

Simple Nine Patch blocks combined with Snowball blocks are a good way to use a novelty fabric in a baby quilt. Keeping a simple color palette of all blues enhances the appealing cowboy print. Any conversation print would be well showcased by this combination of blocks to create a quilt that seems complex but is really quite simple and fun to make. The contrasting red border echoes the kerchiefs of the junior cowboys and creates visual appeal.

Materials

All yardages are based on 42"-wide fabric.

1 yd. theme fabric or novelty print (¾ yd. if you
    do not plan to "fussy cut" the motifs)
¾ yd. dark blue for Snowball block corners
    and outer border
⅜ yd. white print for background of Nine Patch blocks
⅜ yd. blue-and-white check
¼ yd. light blue star print for centers of Nine
    Patch blocks
¼ yd. red for inner border
1½ yds. fabric for backing
½ yd. fabric for binding
42" x 42" batting

Making the Snowball Blocks

1. Using a pencil and your rotary-cutting ruler, draw a diagonal line from corner to corner on the wrong side of the dark blue squares.

2. Place a dark blue square on each corner of a 6½" cowboy-themed square, right sides together. Stitch the blue squares to the cowboy squares along the marked line as shown.

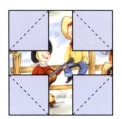

Cutting

Fabric	Used For	Number to Cut	Size to Cut	Second Cut
Dark blue	Snowball blocks	4 strips	2½" x 42"	52 squares, 2½" x 2½"
	Outer border*	4 strips	3½" x 42"	2 strips, 3½" x 33" 2 strips, 3½" x 38½"
Theme fabric	Snowball blocks	13 squares	6½" x 6½"	–
Blue-and-white check	Nine Patch blocks	4 strips	2½" x 42"	–
White print	Background of Nine Patch blocks	4 strips	2½" x 42"	–
Light blue star print	Nine Patch blocks	1 strip	2½" x 42"	–
Red print	Inner border*	4 strips	1½" x 42"	2 strips, 1½" x 30½" 2 strips, 1½" x 33"

* Wait until you have completed the center of the quilt before making the second cut for borders. Measure the quilt through the center and cut the border strips to fit that measurement.

QUILT SIZE: 38" x 38" • BLOCK SIZE: 6"

Designed and pieced by Mary Hickey. Quilted by Dawn Kelly.

3. Align the ¼" line of a rotary-cutting ruler along the seam line of each corner and trim away the excess fabric. Flip open the remaining dark blue triangles and press toward the triangle.

4. Repeat to make 13 blocks.

Make 13.

Making the Nine Patch Blocks

1. Sew a blue-and-white check strip to opposite sides of 2 white print strips. Press toward the blue check strips. Cut the 2 strip sets into a total of 24 segments, each 2½" wide.

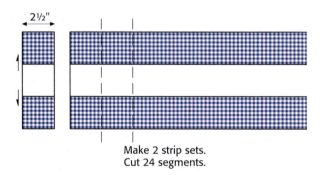

2½"

Make 2 strip sets.
Cut 24 segments.

2. Sew a white print strip to opposite sides of the light blue star print strip. Press toward the light blue print. Cut the strip set into a total of 12 segments, each 2½" wide.

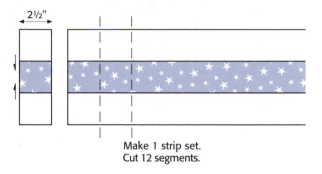

2½"

Make 1 strip set.
Cut 12 segments.

3. Arrange three segments as shown and stitch them to make the Nine Patch block. Repeat to make 12 blocks.

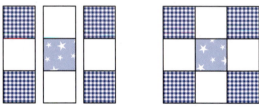

Make 12.

Assembling the Quilt

1. Arrange the blocks in rows, alternating the blocks.

2. Pin at the seam intersections, and sew the blocks together in rows. Press the seams toward the Snowball blocks.

3. Sew the rows together; press the seams all in one direction.

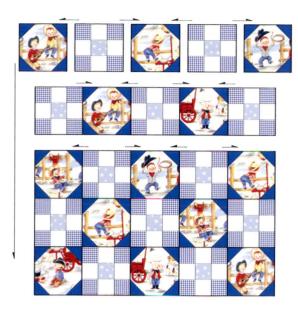

Adding the Borders

Refer to "Borders" on pages 18–19 for more details, if needed. Measure the quilt through the center and cut the border strips to fit that measurement.

1. Sew the inner borders to the sides of the quilt. Press toward the border.

2. Sew the inner borders to the top and bottom of the quilt. Press.

3. Repeat with the outer borders, pressing toward the outer border.

Finishing the Quilt

Refer to the general directions, beginning with "Preparing to Quilt" on page 19, for more details on quilting and finishing.

1. Cut the backing fabric so it is approximately 4" to 6" larger than the quilt top.

2. Layer the backing, batting, and quilt top, and baste the layers together.

3. Hand or machine quilt as desired. The quilt shown was machine quilted with swirls and loops in the blocks and stars and looping lines in the border.

4. Trim the batting and backing fabric so the edges are even with the quilt-top edges, and bind the quilt. Add a hanging sleeve, if desired, and a label.

BABY BOW TIES

One of the most popular quilt block designs in the 1930s was the Bow Tie. The block is easy, fast, and versatile—it can look entirely different in various settings. I, of course, piece the block the easy way without set-in seams, so this is a really fast quilt. I decided to add prairie points to the quilt because they look positively princely and they give the baby something to fondle and finger. Prairie points are simple folded squares stitched to the outer edges of the quilt to add dimension and texture, not to mention a little pizzazz!

Materials

All yardages are based on 42"-wide fabric unless otherwise stated.

¾ yd. light print for block background and plain squares

½ yd. aqua print for prairie points

⅜ yd. or scraps of aqua for blocks

⅜ yd. or scraps of periwinkle for blocks

⅜ yd. blue print for border

¼ yd. or scraps of blue for blocks

1⅛ yds. fabric for backing

32" x 36" batting

Making the Blocks

1. Using a pencil and your rotary-cutting ruler, draw a diagonal line from corner to corner on the wrong side of the blue, aqua, and periwinkle 1½" squares. Lay a marked square on one corner of a 2½" light print square as shown, right sides together. Sew on the marked line. Repeat to make 6 blue units, 18 aqua units, and 18 periwinkle units.

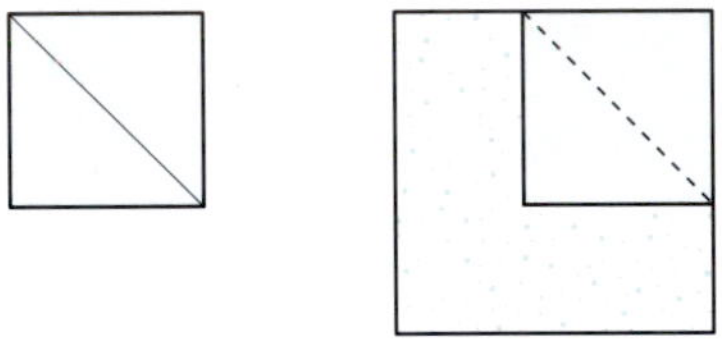

Cutting

Fabric	Used For	Number to Cut	Size to Cut	Second Cut
Blue	Blocks	1 strip	1½" x 21"	6 squares, 1½" x 1½"
		1 strip	2½" x 21"	6 squares, 2½" x 2½"
Aqua	Blocks	2 strips	1½" x 21"	18 squares, 1½" x 1½"
		3 strips	2½" x 21"	18 squares, 2½" x 2½"
Periwinkle	Blocks	2 strips	1½" x 21"	18 squares, 1½" x 1½"
		3 strips	2½" x 21"	18 squares, 2½" x 2½"
Light print	Block background	3 strips	2½" x 42"	42 squares, 2½" x 2½"
	Plain squares	3 strips	4½" x 42"	21 squares, 4½" x 4½"
Blue print	Border*	4 strips	2½" x 42"	4 strips, 2½" x 28½"
Aqua	Prairie points	4 strips	2¾" x 42"	56 squares, 2¾" x 2¾"

* Wait until you have completed the center of the quilt before making the second cut for borders. Measure the quilt through the center and cut the border strips to fit that measurement.

QUILT SIZE: 28" x 32" • BLOCK SIZE: 4"

Designed and pieced by Mary Hickey. Quilted by Frankie Schmitt.

2. Align the ¼" line of a rotary-cutting ruler along the seam line of each unit and trim away the excess fabric. Flip open the remaining colored triangles and press toward the darker fabric.

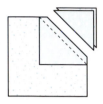

Trim.   Press.

3. Arrange the units from step 2 with the matching 2½" squares to form the blocks as shown. Stitch and press. Make 21 Bow Tie blocks. Press seams toward the darker colors.

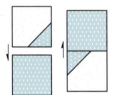

Make 21.

Note from Mary

If you have a friend with breast cancer for whom you would like to make a small quilt, this is a very nice choice. The blocks are quick and easy, the quilt is cheerful and traditional, and creating the bow ties with pink fabric will make it a perfect gift.

Assembling the Quilt Top

1. Stitch the blocks and plain squares together to form 7 rows of 6 blocks each. Press toward the setting squares.

2. Sew the rows together, pressing all the seams in one direction.

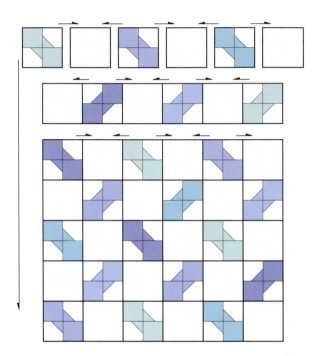

Adding the Border and Prairie Points

Refer to "Borders" on pages 18–19 for more details, if needed. Be sure to measure the quilt top through the center and cut the border strips to fit that measurement.

1. Sew the blue borders to the sides of the quilt. Press toward the border.

2. Sew the blue borders to the top and bottom of the quilt. Press.

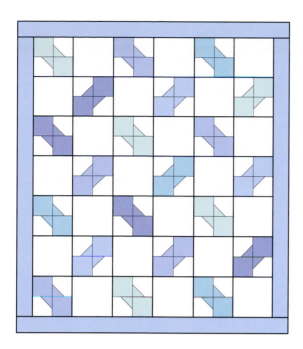

3. Fold each aqua prairie point square in half on the diagonal and on the diagonal again as shown.

Fold.

Fold.

4. Overlapping the edges of the points slightly, pin them, raw edges together, to the quilt top as shown. (At this point, the prairie points should be pointing in toward the center of the quilt.) Pin 15 prairie points to each of the sides and 13 to both the top and bottom of the quilt top.

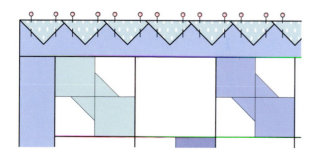

5. Using a scant ¼" seam allowance, carefully stitch the points to the edges of the quilt top, removing the pins as you reach them.

Finishing the Quilt

Refer to the general directions, beginning with "Preparing to Quilt" on page 19, for more details on quilting and finishing.

1. Cut the backing fabric so it is approximately 4" to 6" larger than the quilt top.

2. Layer the backing fabric right sides together with the quilt. Stitch the backing to the quilt top using a ¼" seam and leaving an 8" opening on the bottom edge.

3. Lay the batting over the backing and quilt top, and using the largest stitch length possible, baste the layers together around the outer edges using a scant ¼" seam allowance. Trim the excess backing and batting.

4. Turn the quilt right sides out and smooth the edges and corners. Hand stitch the opening closed.

5. Gently press the quilt and baste the three layers together.

6. Hand or machine quilt as desired. The quilt shown was machine quilted with outline quilting in the blocks, stitching along the printed lines of the fabric in the alternate blocks, and a leaf design in the outer border.

7. Add a hanging sleeve, if desired, and a label.

BRIGHT GARDEN

The Chimney Stone blocks are quick and easy to sew and are combined here with equally simple triangle setting blocks; you can stitch this cheerful quilt in no time to add a bright spot to any baby's room.

Materials

All yardages are based on 42"-wide fabric.
1 yd. bright green for setting blocks and outer border
¾ yd. white print for background of Chimney Stone blocks
⅝ yd. light green check for setting blocks

⅜ yd. dark green for Chimney Stone blocks and accent border
¼ yd. red for Chimney Stone blocks
¼ yd. blue for Chimney Stone blocks
¼ yd. yellow for Chimney Stone blocks
1½ yds. fabric for backing
⅜ yd. fabric for binding
40" x 40" batting

Cutting

Fabric	Used For	Number to Cut	Size to Cut	Second Cut
White	Chimney Stone blocks	4 strips	1½" x 42"	–
		3 strips	2½" x 42"	Cut in half to make a total of 6 strips, 2½" x 21".
		2 strips	2½" x 42"	28 squares, 2½" x 2½"
	Border corner blocks	2 strips	1½" x 42"	6 strips, 1½" x 9"
Red	Chimney Stone blocks	1 strip	1½" x 42"	–
		1 strip	2½" x 21"	–
	Border corner blocks	1 strip	1½" x 9"	–
Blue	Chimney Stone blocks	1 strip	1½" x 42"	–
		1 strip	2½" x 21"	–
	Border corner blocks	1 strip	1½" x 9"	–
Yellow	Chimney Stone blocks	1 strip	1½" x 42"	–
		1 strip	2½" x 21"	–
	Border corner blocks	1 strip	1½" x 9"	–
Dark green	Chimney Stone blocks	1 strip	1½" x 42"	–
		1 square	2½" x 2½"	–
	Accent border	4 strips	1" x 42"	–
Light green check	Setting blocks	4 squares	7" x 7"	–
		1 square	7¼" x 7¼"	–
Bright green	Setting blocks	6 squares	7" x 7"	–
		1 square	7¼" x 7¼"	–
	Outer border*	4 strips	3½" x 42"	4 strips, 3½" x 30½"

* Wait until you have completed the center of the quilt before making the second cut for borders. Measure the quilt through the center and cut the border strips to fit that measurement.

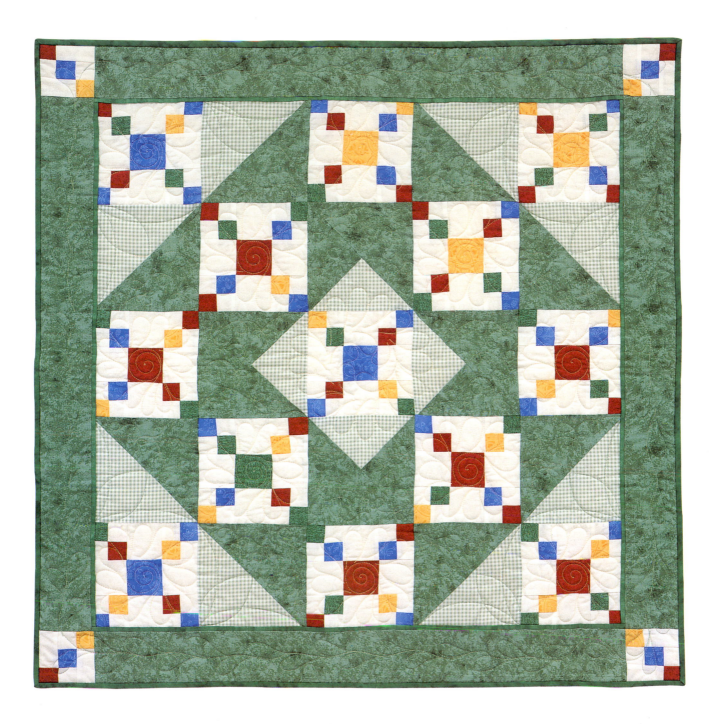

Q UILT SIZE: 36" x 36" • B LOCK SIZE: 6"

Designed and pieced by Mary Hickey. Quilted by Dawn Kelly.

Making the Chimney Stone Blocks

1. Sew a 1½" x 42" white strip to each of the red, blue, yellow, and dark green strips as shown. Cut each strip set into 26 segments, 1½" wide, for a total of 104 segments.

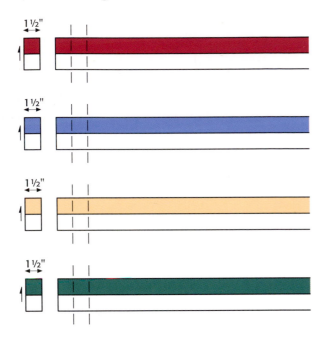

2. Randomly alternate the colors and sew the segments together to make 52 four-patch units.

Make 52.

3. Sew a 2½" x 21" white strip on opposite sides of the 2½" x 21" red, blue, and yellow strips to make the short strip sets. (*Note:* You will use the one 2½" green square to make a single block with a green square in the center.)

4. Cut the short strip sets into a total of 12 segments, 2½" wide.

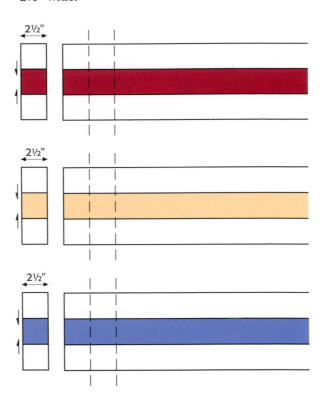

5. Arrange the four-patch units, 2½" white squares, and strip set segments as shown to make the blocks. Sew the units together to make 13 Chimney Stone blocks. (Make one using the 2½" green square in the center.)

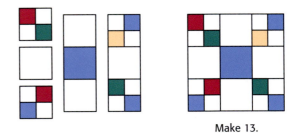

Make 13.

Making the Triangle Blocks

1. Layer the 4 light green check 7" squares and the 4 bright green 7" squares in pairs, right sides together, with the lighter color on top. Using a pencil and your rotary-cutting ruler, draw a

diagonal line through the center of each light green square. Draw another line ¼" away on both sides of the first line.

2. Stitch on the second and third drawn lines. Cut along the center line, flip open the squares, and press toward the darker fabric. Make 8 triangle squares as shown. Measure and trim them to 6½" square.

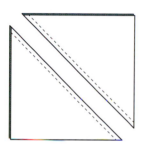

Make 8.

Making the Corner Triangle Blocks

1. Layer the remaining 2 bright green 7" squares and cut them once on the diagonal. Set these triangles aside.

2. Layer the bright green 7¼" square and the light green check 7¼" square, right sides together, with the lighter color on top. Using a pencil and your rotary-cutting ruler, draw a diagonal line through the center of the light green square. Draw another line ¼" away on both sides of the first line. Stitch on the second and third drawn lines.

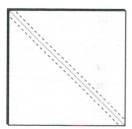

3. Cut along the center line, flip open the squares, and press toward the darker fabric.

4. Cut the sewn squares once on the diagonal.

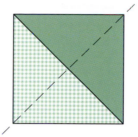 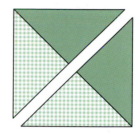

5. Assemble the triangles from step 1 and the units from step 4 to make 4 corner blocks. Measure the squares and trim to 6½" x 6½".

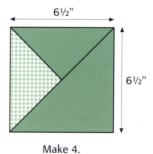

Make 4.

Making the Border Corner Blocks

1. Make 3 strip sets using the 1½" x 9" red, blue, and yellow strips with 1½"-wide and 2½"-wide white strips as shown.

2. Cut each strip set into 4 segments, 1½" wide.

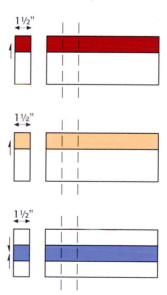

3. Assemble into 4 little Nine Patch–style blocks for the outer border corners.

Make 4.

Assembling the Quilt

1. Arrange the blocks in rows, alternating the blocks as shown.

2. Sew the blocks together in rows, pressing the seams toward the setting blocks.

3. Sew the rows together, pressing the seams all in one direction.

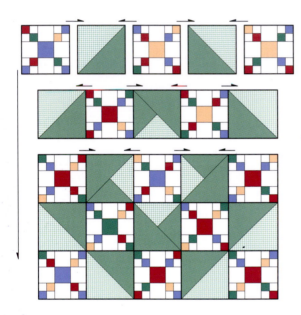

Adding the Borders

Refer to "Borders" on pages 18–19 for more details, if needed. Measure the quilt top through the center and cut the border strips to fit that measurement.

1. Cut the dark green 1" strips to fit the measurements of the quilt top. Fold the strips in half, wrong sides together, and press.

2. With raw edges together, stitch 2 of the strips to the sides of the quilt top. The green will overlap the blocks, slightly hiding the edges of the quilt.

3. With raw edges together, stitch the remaining 2 strips to the top and bottom of the quilt.

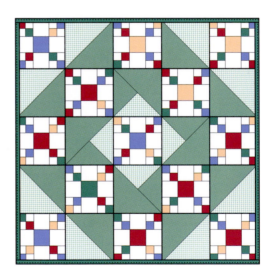

4. Sew 2 outer border strips to the sides of the quilt, pressing toward the outer borders.

5. Stitch the Nine Patch blocks to the ends of the remaining outer border strips.

6. Sew the outer border units to the top and bottom of the quilt. Press.

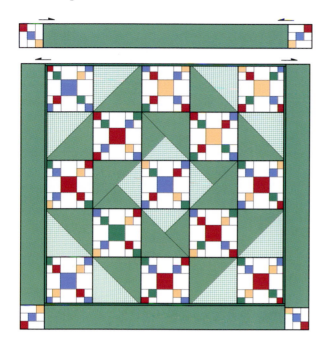

Finishing the Quilt

Refer to the general directions, beginning with "Preparing to Quilt" on page 19, for more details on quilting and finishing.

1. Cut the backing fabric so it is approximately 4" to 6" larger than the quilt top.

2. Layer the backing, batting, and quilt top, and baste the layers together.

3. Hand or machine quilt as desired. The quilt shown was machine quilted with feathered wreaths in the Chimney Stone blocks, petals and leaves in the setting blocks, and a leaf design in the border.

4. Trim the batting and backing fabric so the edges are even with the quilt top edges, and bind the quilt. Add a hanging sleeve, if desired, and a label.

HEART IN THE GARDEN

For a super fast Valentine's Day quilt, consider making the Chimney Stone blocks in two colors and using just four fabrics in the whole quilt. In the middle of the quilt, use a plain white square and appliqué a single heart onto it.

PETITE BOUQUETS

This beloved old block, the Churn Dash, has always been one of my favorites. It conjures memories of our pioneer grandmothers working on the farm to feed and shelter their families. My daughter and I have made it many times for very special gifts and no matter what color scheme we use, it always creates a wonderful quilt with a warm cuddly feel. I used a larger-scale block for this quilt, which makes it both attractive as a wall quilt and useful as a practical baby quilt. Although this quilt is fairly large, you could choose to make only four or six blocks for a smaller quilt.

Materials

All yardages are based on 42"-wide fabric.

1 yd. green for blocks and sashing

1 yd. red for triangles and outer border

⅝ yd. light print for block background

½ yd. floral bouquet print for block centers* and cornerstones

2⅜ yds. fabric for backing

½ yd. fabric for binding

51" x 51" batting

* This quilt contains a 3" square that features dainty little bouquets. The motifs were far apart and I wanted them to be centered in the squares, so I had to "fussy cut" them. If you plan to fussy cut you may need to purchase extra fabric, and you should not cut the floral fabric into strips as directed in the cutting chart. See page 9 for more information on fussy cutting.

Making the Blocks

1. Sew 2 strip sets using 2" x 42" strips of light print and green. Press toward the green. Cut the strip sets into 18 segments, 3½" wide.

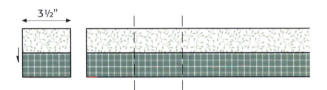

Cutting

Fabric	Used For	Number to Cut	Size to Cut	Second Cut
Light print	Rectangles in blocks	4 strips	2" x 42"	–
	Triangles in blocks	2 strips	4" x 42"	18 squares, 4" x 4"
Green	Rectangles in blocks	4 strips	2" x 42"	–
	Sashing	6 strips	3½" x 42"	24 rectangles, 3½" x 9½"
Floral bouquet	Block centers	1 strip	3½" x 42"	9 squares, 3½" x 3½"
	Cornerstones	2 strips	3½" x 42"	16 squares, 3½" x 3½"
Red	Triangles in blocks	2 strips	4" x 42"	18 squares, 4" x 4"
	Outer border*	5 strips	4¼" x 42"	2 strips, 4¼" x 39½"
				2 strips, 4¼" x 47"

* Wait until you have completed the center of the quilt before making the second cut and piecing the borders. Measure the quilt through the center. Cut and piece the border strips as needed to fit that measurement.

QUILT SIZE: 46½" x 46½" • BLOCK SIZE: 9"

Designed and pieced by Mary Hickey. Quilted by Amanda Miller.

2. Sew a strip set using the following strips in the order listed. If you are fussy cutting, make 2 strip sets using the light print and green 2" x 42" strips, cut the strip sets into 18 segments, 3½" wide, and go to step 4. Press the seams toward the green.

    2" x 42" light print

    2" x 42" green

    3½" x 42" floral bouquet

    2" x 42" green

    2" x 42" light print

3. Cut the strip set into 9 segments, 3½" wide.

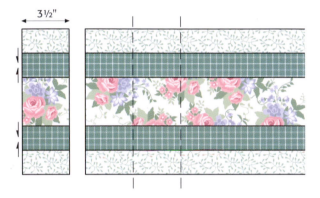

Mary's Helpful Hint

If you are fussy cutting the center motifs, you will cut the center pieces into 3½" squares and assemble them in columns with the light print and green segments as shown.

Fussy-Cutting Option

4. Layer the 18 light print and red squares in pairs, right sides together, with the light print on top. Using a pencil and a rotary-cutting ruler, draw a diagonal line through the center of the light print square. Draw a second line ¼" to the left of the first line. Draw a third line ¼" to the right of the first line. Stitch along the second and third lines.

5. Cut along the first line, flip the triangles open, and press toward the darker fabric. Measure and trim the squares to 3½". Make 36 half-square triangles.

Make 36.

6. Arrange the units to form the Churn Dash blocks. Sew the units together to make 9 blocks.

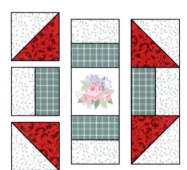

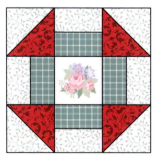

Make 9.

Assembling the Quilt Top

1. Stitch the blocks together with sashings to form 3 rows of 3 blocks and 4 sashing pieces each as shown. Press toward the sashing.

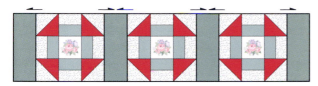

Make 3.

2. Assemble the sashings and cornerstones to form 4 rows of 3 sashing pieces and 4 cornerstones each as shown. Press.

Make 4.

3. Sew the rows together with the sashing-and-cornerstone strips between them.

4. Sew rows of sashing pieces and cornerstones to the top and bottom of the quilt top.

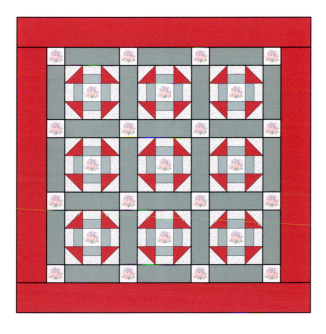

Adding the Borders

Refer to "Borders" on pages 18–19 for more details, if needed. Measure the quilt top through the center and cut the side border strips to fit that measurement. Measure again to piece and cut the top and bottom borders.

1. Sew the 4¼" outer border strips to the sides of the quilt top. Press toward the outer border.

2. Sew the 4¼" outer border strips to the top and bottom of the quilt. Press.

Finishing the Quilt

Refer to the general directions, beginning with "Preparing to Quilt" on page 19, for more details on quilting and finishing.

1. Cut the backing fabric so it is approximately 4" to 6" larger than the quilt top.

2. Layer the backing, batting, and quilt top, and baste the layers together.

3. Hand or machine quilt as desired. The quilt shown was hand quilted with outline quilting in the blocks, cable designs in the sashings, and a twisted ribbon in the outer border.

4. Trim the batting and backing fabric so the edges are even with the quilt-top edges, and bind the quilt. Add a hanging sleeve, if desired, and a label.

LITTLE BUDDY

This little quilt is a companion to the "Baby Baskets" quilt shown on page 78. Make the basket quilt to hang on the nursery wall and use this hard-working piece for the real purposes of a baby quilt—cuddling, burping, drooling, and all-around comforting. The multifaceted look of a large, serious quilt is packed into this diminutive version. The quilt looks intricate and old-fashioned, but the blocks are small and quick to sew, making this a good quilt for constant use or for when you need to whip one up in a hurry. Look for two shades of green and three shades of peach.

Materials

All yardages are based on 42"-wide fabric.

¾ yd. light green for Hourglass blocks and outer border

½ yd. dark green for Hourglass blocks and inner border

⅜ yd. medium peach for framing triangles

¼ yd. light peach for Four Patch blocks

¼ yd. dark peach for Four Patch blocks

1 yd. fabric for backing

⅜ yd. fabric for binding

34" x 34" batting

Making the Framed Four Patch Blocks

1. Stitch the light peach and dark peach strips together in pairs to make 2 strip sets. Press toward the darker color. Cut into 26 segments, 2" wide.

Cutting

Fabric	Used For	Number to Cut	Size to Cut	Second Cut
Light peach	Four Patch blocks	2 strips	2" x 42"	–
Dark peach	Four Patch blocks	2 strips	2" x 42"	–
Medium peach	Framing triangles	2 strips	3" x 42"	26 squares, 3" x 3"; cut diagonally once to make 52 triangles.
Light green	Hourglass blocks	1 strip	5½" x 42"	6 squares, 5½" x 5½"
	Outer borders*	4 strips	3½" x 42"	2 strips. 3½" x 23¾" 2 strips, 3½" x 29¾"
Dark green	Hourglass blocks	1 strip	5½" x 42"	6 squares, 5½" x 5½"
	Inner borders*	4 strips	1½" x 42"	2 strips, 1½" x 21¾" 2 strips, 1½" x 23¾"

* Wait until you have completed the center of the quilt before making the second cut for borders. Measure the quilt through the center and cut the border strips to fit that measurement.

QUILT SIZE: 29¼" x 29¼" • BLOCK SIZE: 4¼"

Designed and pieced by Mary Hickey. Quilted by Dawn Kelly.

2. Stitch the segments together, alternating colors, to make the four-patch units. Make 13.

Make 13.

3. Stitch the medium peach triangles to the edges of the four-patch units to make 13 framed Four Patch blocks as shown. Press toward the triangles.

Make 13.

Making the Hourglass Blocks

1. Layer the light green and dark green squares in pairs, right sides together, with the lighter square on top. Using a pencil and your rotary-cutting ruler, draw a diagonal line through the center of the light green square as shown. Draw a second line ¼" to the left of the first line. Draw a third line ¼" to the right of the first line.

2. Stitch along the second and third lines.

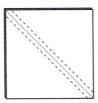

3. Cut along the first line. Flip the triangles open and press toward the darker color.

 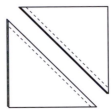

4. Cut the sewn squares on the diagonal to make 2 triangle pieces from each square.

5. Assemble the triangle pairs; stitch to make 12 Hourglass blocks, and press. Measure the blocks and trim to 4¾" x 4¾".

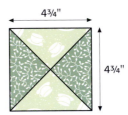

Make 12.

Assembling the Quilt

1. Arrange the blocks in 5 rows of 5 blocks each, alternating the blocks and orienting the framed Four Patch blocks as shown.

2. Sew the blocks together in rows, pressing the seams toward the Hourglass blocks.

3. Sew the rows together, pressing the seams all in one direction.

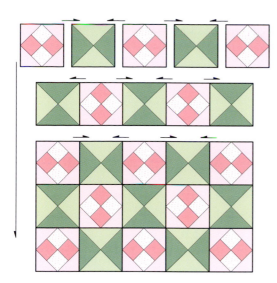

Adding the Borders

Refer to "Borders" on pages 18–19 for more details, if needed. Measure the quilt through the center and cut the border strips to fit that measurement.

1. Sew the inner borders to the sides of the quilt. Press toward the border.

2. Sew the inner borders to the top and bottom of the quilt. Press.

3. Repeat with the outer borders, pressing toward the outer border.

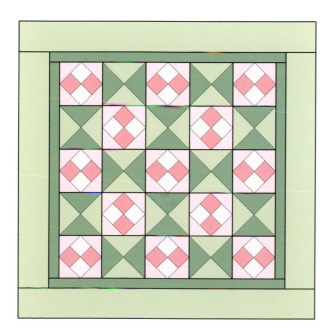

Finishing the Quilt

Refer to the general directions, beginning with "Preparing to Quilt" on page 19, for more details on quilting and finishing.

1. Cut the backing fabric so it is approximately 4" to 6" larger than the quilt top.

2. Layer the backing, batting, and quilt top, and baste the layers together.

3. Hand or machine quilt as desired. The quilt shown was machine quilted with petal shapes in the blocks and a leaf pattern in the borders.

4. Trim the batting and backing fabric so the edges are even with the quilt-top edges, and bind the quilt. Add a hanging sleeve, if desired, and a label.

Note from Mary

If you have a friend with breast cancer for whom you would like to make a small quilt, this is a very nice choice. The blocks are quick and easy, the quilt is cheerful and traditional, and the pink four-patch units resemble small pink bows.

PLAYMATES

I love making this quilt as a gift because it is so simple to stitch and yet it looks like an honest-to-goodness serious quilt—cleverly giving the recipient the idea that I spent many hard hours working away on behalf of her new baby. The blocks are pretty and give that multifaceted look we so love in any quilt. This particular novelty fabric even had a companion border, so I took advantage of these fabrics in the quilt's quick-and-easy design. A single row of red rickrack tucked in the binding adds a bit of fun and texture.

Materials

All yardages are based on 42"-wide fabric.

⅞ yd. novelty border print for outer border

⅝ yd. novelty fabric for Snowball blocks

¼ yd. dark pink for Hourglass blocks, inner border, and outer border corners

½ yd. light pink for Hourglass blocks

¼ yd. rose for Snowball block corners

1⅛ yds. fabric for backing

⅜ yd. fabric for binding

35" x 35" batting

2 packages of jumbo red rickrack (3½ yds.)

Making the Snowball Blocks

1. Using a pencil and your rotary-cutting ruler, draw a diagonal line from corner to corner on the wrong side of the rose squares. Lay a marked square on each corner of a novelty square, right sides together. Stitch along the diagonal line.

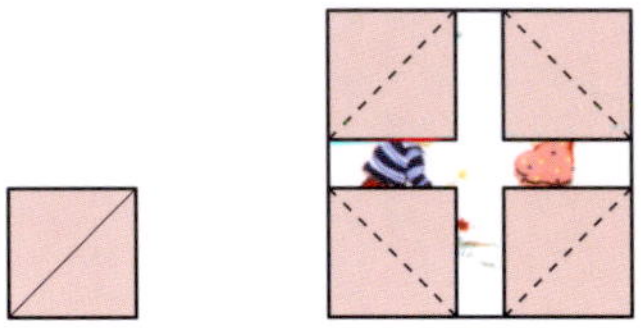

Cutting

Fabric	Used For	Number to Cut	Size to Cut	Second Cut
Rose	Corners of Snowball blocks	3 strips	2" x 42"	52 squares, 2" x 2"
Novelty fabric	Snowball blocks	2 strips	4¾" x 42"	13 squares, 4¾" x 4¾"
Light pink	Hourglass blocks	1 strip	5½" x 42"	6 squares, 5½" x 5½"
Dark pink	Hourglass blocks	1 strip	5½" x 42"	6 squares, 5½" x 5½"
	Inner border*	4 strips	1½" x 42"	2 strips 1½" x 21¾"
				2 strips, 1½" x 23¾"
	Corners of outer borders	4 squares	4¼" x 4¼"	—
Novelty border print	Outer border*	4 strips	4¼" x 42"	4 strips, 4¼" x 23¾"

* Wait until you have completed the center of the quilt before making the second cut for borders. Measure the quilt through the center and cut the border strips to fit that measurement.

QUILT SIZE: 30¾" x 30¾" • BLOCK SIZE: 4¼"

Designed and pieced by Mary Hickey. Quilted by Frankie Schmitt.

2. Align the ¼" line of a rotary-cutting ruler along the seam line of each unit and trim away the excess fabric. Flip open the remaining rose triangles and press seams toward the triangle. Repeat to make 13 Snowball blocks.

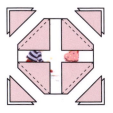

Make 13.

Making the Hourglass Blocks

1. Layer the light pink and dark pink squares in pairs, right sides together, with the lighter square on top. Using a pencil and your rotary-cutting ruler, draw a diagonal line through the center of the light pink square as shown. Draw a second line ¼" to the left of the first line. Draw a third line ¼" to the right of the first line.

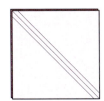

2. Stitch along the second and third lines. Cut along the first line.

 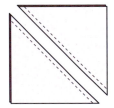

3. Flip the triangles open and press toward the darker color.

4. Cut the sewn squares on the diagonal to make 2 triangle units from each square.

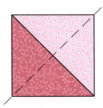 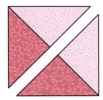

5. Sew the triangle units together and press. Measure the blocks and trim to 4¾" x 4¾". Make 12 Hourglass blocks.

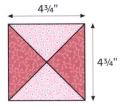

Make 12.

Assembling the Quilt

1. Arrange the blocks in 5 rows of 5 blocks each, alternating the blocks as shown.

2. Sew the blocks together in rows, pressing the seams toward the Hourglass blocks.

3. Sew the rows together, pressing the seams all in one direction.

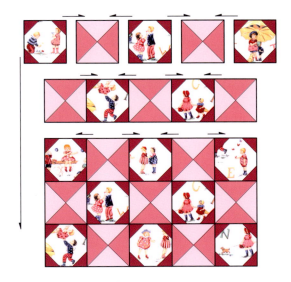

Adding the Borders

Refer to "Borders" on pages 18–19 for more details, if needed. Measure the quilt through the center and cut the border strips to fit that measurement.

1. Sew the inner borders to the sides of the quilt. Press toward the border.

2. Sew the inner borders to the top and bottom of the quilt. Press.

3. Sew the outer borders to the sides of the quilt. Press toward the outer border.

4. Sew the dark pink squares to the ends of the novelty borders for the top and bottom of the quilt.

5. Stitch the top and bottom border units to the quilt. Press.

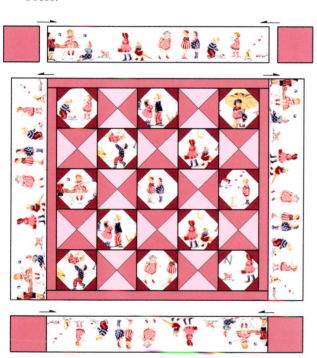

Finishing the Quilt

Refer to the general directions, beginning with "Preparing to Quilt" on page 19, for more details on quilting and finishing.

1. Cut the backing fabric so it is approximately 4" to 6" larger than the quilt top.

2. Layer the backing, batting, and quilt top, and baste the layers together.

3. Hand or machine quilt as desired. The quilt shown was machine quilted with petal shapes in the blocks and free motion quilting around the designs in the novelty fabrics.

4. Trim the batting and backing fabric so their edges are even with the quilt-top edges.

5. Using a longer stitch length, baste the rickrack to the edges of the top of the quilt. It should be centered on the ¼" seam line for the binding.

6. Layer the binding over the rickrack and sew it to the quilt. Fold the binding to the back of the quilt and blind stitch it in place.

7. Add a hanging sleeve, if desired, and a label.

FAMILY HEARTS

In this quilt, bright hearts dance joyfully around a small star, surrounding it with love and happiness. The little star has the baby's name on it, and each heart has the name of a family member on it. This turns the quilt into a family tree for the new arrival, with each heart representing someone who loves and cherishes the baby.

*   With this quilt, we also made a special heart album for our baby. Each page in the book has a heart corresponding to one in the quilt and, next to it, a photograph of the relative whose name is on the quilt. We had the book laminated (drool-proofed) and bound at an office supply store, making it a practical and safe album for the baby to hold, chew on, and treasure.*

Materials

All yardages are based on 42"-wide fabric unless otherwise stated.

1 yd. white for block background

⅝ yd. blue for border

½ yd. blue-and-white striped fabric for sashings

¼ yd. each or scraps of 8 or 10 bright colors for heart, stars, and cornerstones

2 yds. fabric for backing

½ yd. fabric for binding

45" x 45" batting

Lightweight interfacing for appliqué

Hearts and Stars Appliqué

In this quilt, I hemmed the hearts with what I call the "face-and-turn" method. I prefer this method because it is slightly faster than fusing and it gives you a finished edge. You can fuse the hearts once they are hemmed or you can hand or machine appliqué them. For the facing of the shapes, I prefer a lightweight "sew-in" interfacing but not the very thinnest one—the one called feather-to-medium weight. Set the stitch length on your sewing machine to a very short stitch.

1. Cut squares of fabric 6", 4", or 3" in the colors you choose for your hearts and star.

2. Make templates using the patterns on pages 68 and 69. Using the templates, draw the hearts and star on a piece of featherweight interfacing with a blue

Cutting

Fabric	Used For	Number to Cut	Size to Cut	Second Cut
Bright-colored scraps	Hearts	29	Heart template (page 69)	—
	Star	1	Star template (page 68)	—
	Cornerstones	16 squares	2" x 2"	—
White	Block backgrounds	9 squares	10" x 10"	—
Blue-and-white stripe	Sashings	6 strips	2" x 42"	24 rectangles, 2" x 10"
Blue	Border*	4 strips	3¾" x 42"	2 strips, 3¾" x 35" 2 strips, 3¾" x 41½"

* Wait until you have completed the center of the quilt before making the second cut for borders. Measure the quilt through the center and cut the border strips to fit that measurement.

QUILT SIZE: 41" x 41" • BLOCK SIZE: 9½"

Designed, pieced, and appliquéd by Mary Hickey. Quilted by Dawn Kelly.

water-soluble pen. Cut out the shapes, leaving about ½" around the edges for seam allowance.

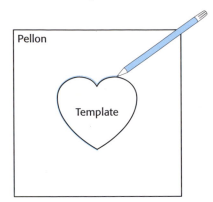

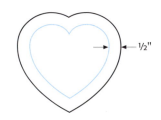

3. Pin the Pellon shapes to the right side of the heart fabrics.

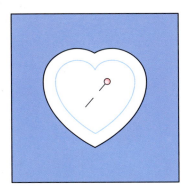

4. Set your sewing machine to a very short stitch length, about 1.0 on a European machine and 18 on an American machine.

5. Stitch on the drawn line of each shape using the tiny stitches. When you come to the **V** of the heart, stop the machine with the needle down, pivot the fabric, take two stitches across, stop again with the needle down, pivot again, and then start sewing up the other side of the heart, as shown. This will enable you to turn the heart smoothly with no puckers. Overlap the stitching when you reach your starting point.

6. Trim the seam allowance to a scant ⅛". Cut a slit in the interfacing about 1½" long. Make a careful snip at the inner point of the heart as shown.

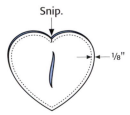

7. Spritz the heart with a spray bottle of water to remove the blue lines.

8. While the heart is still wet, turn it right side out and use a knitting needle to smooth out the outer edges.

9. Press the shapes and position them on the blocks. Pin or baste them to the background fabric.

10. Hand stitch, machine stitch, or fuse the hearts in place on the blocks. Refer to "Appliqué Primer" on pages 13–16.

Assembling the Quilt

1. Stitch the blocks together with sashings to form 3 rows of 3 blocks and 2 sashing pieces each as shown. **Press toward the sashing strips.**

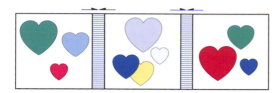

2. Assemble the sashings and cornerstones to form 4 rows of 3 sashing pieces and 2 cornerstones. Press toward the sashing.

3. Sew the rows together with the sashing-and-cornerstone strips between them. Sew rows of sashing pieces and cornerstones to the top and bottom of the quilt top.

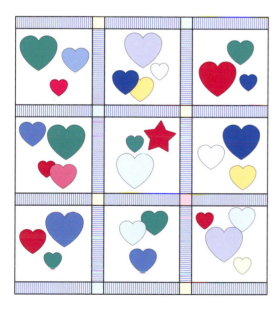

4. Make 2 rows of 3 sashing pieces and 4 cornerstones each, and sew to the sides.

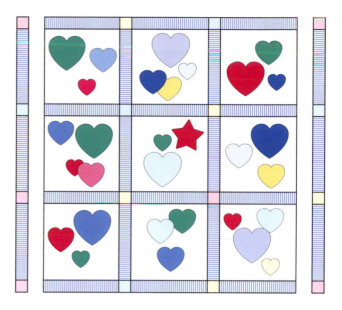

Adding the Borders

Refer to "Borders" on pages 18–19 for more details, if needed. Be sure to measure the quilt top through the center and cut the border strips to fit that measurement.

1. Sew the outer borders to the sides of the quilt top. Press the seams toward the outer border.

2. Sew the outer borders to the top and bottom of the quilt. Press.

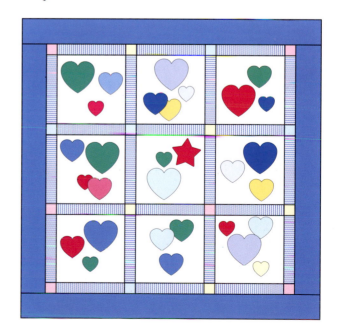

Finishing the Quilt

Refer to the general directions, beginning with "Preparing to Quilt" on page 19, for more details on quilting and finishing.

1. Cut the backing fabric so it is approximately 4" to 6" larger than the quilt top.

2. Layer the backing, batting, and quilt top, and baste the layers together.

3. Hand or machine quilt as desired. The quilt shown was machine quilted with echo quilting around all the shapes in the blocks, cable designs in the sashings, and a twisted ribbon in the outer border.

4. Trim the batting and backing fabric so the edges are even with the quilt-top edges, and bind the quilt. Add a hanging sleeve, if desired, and a label.

Star
Cut 1.

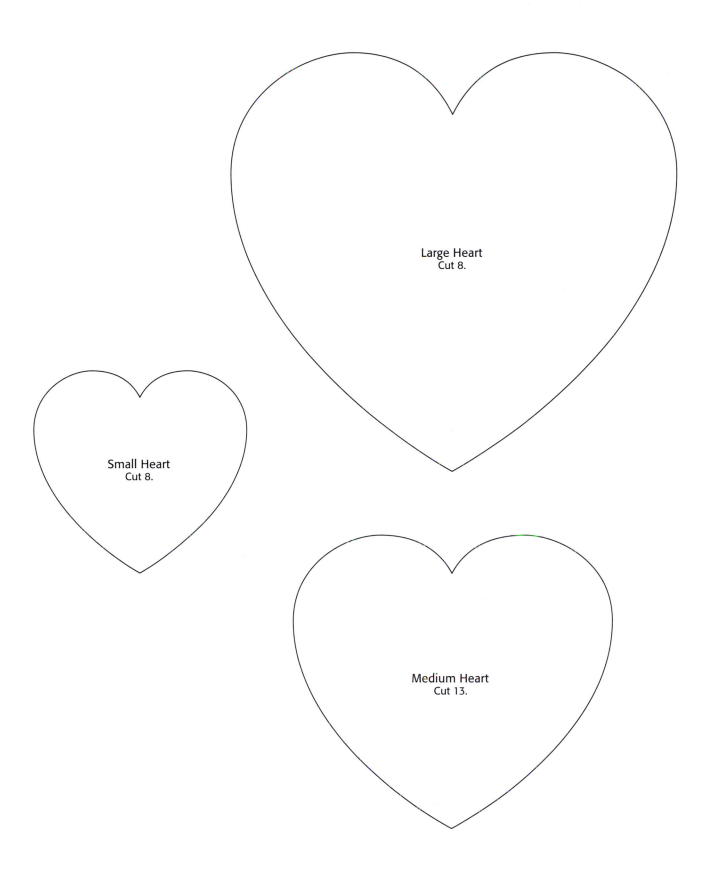

Large Heart
Cut 8.

Small Heart
Cut 8.

Medium Heart
Cut 13.

WIGGLE FLOWERS

The sweet colors of the 1930s-style fabrics and the mischievous wiggle of the stems give this quilt its friendly charm. Plump, cheerful little flowers are sure to bring out a smile when you wrap the baby in this quilt. You can fuse the shapes to the background and then stitch them with a straight, zigzag, or blanket stitch. I chose to set the blocks in three vertical rows with a zigzag setting to add even more personality to this playful block.

Materials

All yardages are based on 42"-wide fabric unless otherwise stated.

¾ yd. light blue for setting triangles

⅝ yd. medium blue print for border

½ yd. white for block background

⅛ yd. each or scraps of 11 different 1930s-style fabrics for blocks

⅛ yd. each or scraps of 3 different 1930s-style greens for appliqué

1½ yds. fabric for backing

⅜ yd. fabric for binding

37" x 45" batting

Fusible web

Making the Blocks

1. Using a pencil and your rotary-cutting ruler, draw a diagonal line from corner to corner on the wrong side of the 1930s-style squares. Lay a marked square on one corner of a white square as shown, right sides together. Sew on the marked line. Repeat to make 11 units.

 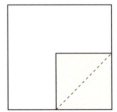

Cutting

Fabric	Used For	Number to Cut	Size to Cut	Second Cut
White	Background	2 strips	6½" x 42"	11 squares, 6½" x 6½"
1930s-style fabrics	Flower petals	33	Petal template (page 73)	—
	Flower pots	11 squares	3½" x 3½"	—
1930s-style green fabrics	Leaves	22	Leaf template (page 73)	—
Light blue	Corner triangles	4 strips	5¼" x 42"	22 squares, 5¼" x 5¼"; cut each square once diagonally to make 44 corner triangles.
	Center vertical row*	2 rectangles	4¾" x 9"	—
Medium blue	Border†	4	4" x 42"	2 strips, 4" x 34½" 2 strips, 4" x 41½"

* These can be cut from the leftover 5¼" strip cut for the corner triangles.

† Wait until you have completed the center of the quilt before cutting the border strips. Measure the quilt through the center and cut the border strips to fit that measurement.

QUILT SIZE: 32½" x 41" • BLOCK SIZE: 6"

Designed, pieced, and appliquéd by Mary Hickey. Quilted by Dawn Kelly.

2. Align the ¼" line of a rotary-cutting ruler along the seam line of each unit and trim away the excess fabric. Flip open the remaining 1930s-style triangles and press toward the darker colors.

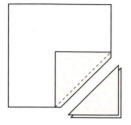 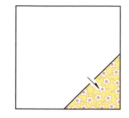

Appliquéing the Blocks

1. Make templates from the petal and leaf patterns on page 73. Trace the shapes onto the fusible web and fuse to the wrong sides of the appliqué fabrics. Cut out and appliqué the petals and leaves to the blocks. See "Appliqué Primer" on pages 13–16 for more details, if needed.

2. Using a pencil, trace the stem onto each block using the block diagram on page 73. Embroider the stem by hand or by using the zigzag stitch on your sewing machine.

Assembling the Quilt

1. Stitch 4 light blue corner triangles to each block. Make 11 blocks.

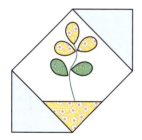 

Make 11.

2. Stitch a light blue rectangle to the top of one of the blocks. Stitch the second blue rectangle to the bottom of another block.

3. Sew the blocks together in 3 vertical rows, as shown.

4. Sew the rows together; press toward the light blue triangles.

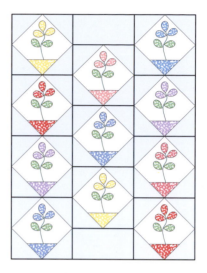

Adding the Borders

Refer to "Borders" on pages 18–19 for more details, if needed. Measure the quilt through the center and cut the border strips to fit that measurement.

1. Sew the border strips to the sides of the quilt, and press the seams toward the border.

2. Sew the border strips to the top and bottom of the quilt and press.

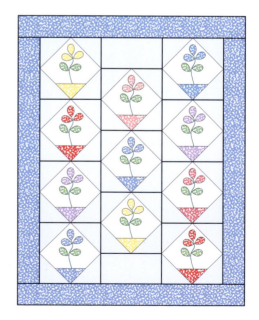

Finishing the Quilt

Refer to the general directions beginning with "Preparing to Quilt" on page 19 for more details on quilting and finishing.

1. Cut the backing fabric so it is approximately 4" to 6" larger than the quilt top.

2. Layer the backing, batting, and quilt top, and baste the layers together.

3. Hand or machine quilt as desired. The quilt shown was quilted with outline and stipple quilting in the blocks, a vine design in the setting triangles, and a loop pattern in the borders.

4. Trim the batting and backing fabric so the edges are even with the quilt-top edges, and bind the quilt. Add a hanging sleeve, if desired, and a label.

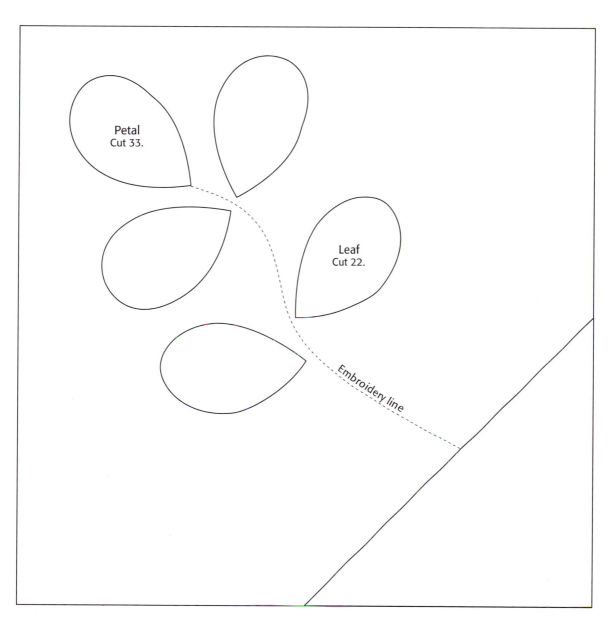

Petal
Cut 33.

Leaf
Cut 22.

Embroidery line

Appliqué Patterns and Placement Diagram

SUNNY SAILORS

You can almost feel the sun on your shoulders and the breeze in the baby's hair (if he has any!) when you see this happy quilt. Sailboats have always been a favorite design for baby quilts. This quilt is a creative twist on an old favorite: first we added yellow and then we tipped the sailboats in the evening breeze. In this quilt I swapped the traditional red, white, and blue color scheme for one of yellow, white, and blue. Placing the block on tilted triangles puts the quilt into a gentle motion. This is a fairly large quilt, but you can easily change it to 9 or 16 blocks if you prefer a smaller version.

Materials

All yardages are based on 42"-wide fabric unless otherwise stated.

1¼ yds. blue cloud fabric for block corners and outer border

1⅛ yds. blue-and-yellow print for setting squares

¾ yd. light blue print for block background

⅜ yd. white for sails

⅜ yd. yellow for inner border

¼ yd. or scraps of yellow for boat hulls

2¼ yds. fabric for backing

½ yd. fabric for binding

54" x 54" batting

Cutting

Fabric	Used For	Number to Cut	Size to Cut	Second Cut
Light blue print	Background of boat blocks	2 strips	2½" x 42"	24 squares, 2½" x 2½"
		1 strip	3½" x 42"	6 squares, 3½" x 3½"
		1 strip	4" x 42"	6 squares, 4 " x 4"
		5 strips	1" x 42"	12 pieces, 1" x 4" 12 pieces, 1" x 3½" 12 pieces, 1" x 6½"
		1 strip	1½" x 42"	12 pieces, 1½" x 3"
White	Sails	1 strip	3½" x 42"	6 squares, 3½" x 3½"
		1 strip	4" x 42"	6 squares, 4" x 4"
Yellow scraps	Boat hulls	12 rectangles	2½" x 6½"	—
Blue cloud	Tilting corners	5 strips	3" x 42"	24 rectangles, 3" x 7⅛"
	Outer border*	5 strips	4" x 42"	2 strips, 4" x 43" 2 strips, 4" x 50"
Blue-and-yellow print	Setting squares	4 strips	8½" x 42"	13 squares, 8½" x 8½"
Yellow	Inner border*	5 strips	1¾" x 42"	2 strips, 1¾" x 40½" 2 strips, 1¾" x 43"

* Wait until you have completed the center of the quilt before piecing and making the second cut for the borders. Measure the quilt through the center. Cut and piece the border strips as needed to fit that measurement.

QUILT SIZE: 49½" x 49½" • BLOCK SIZE: 8"

Designed and pieced by Mary Hickey. Quilted by Dawn Kelly.

Making the Small Sails

1. Layer the 3½" light blue squares and the 3½" white squares in pairs, right sides together, with the white square on top. Using a pencil and your rotary-cutting ruler, draw a diagonal line through the center of the white square. Draw a second line ¼" to the left of the first line. Draw a third line ¼" to the right of the first line. Stitch along the second and third lines, and cut along the first line.

2. Flip the triangles open and press toward the light blue. Measure and trim the blocks to 3" square.

Make 12.

Making the Large Sails

1. Layer the 4" light blue squares and the 4" white squares in pairs, right sides together, with the white square on top. Using a pencil and your rotary-cutting ruler, draw a diagonal line through the center of the white square. Draw a second line ¼" to the left of the first line. Draw a third line ¼" to the right of the first line. Stitch along the second and third lines, and cut along the first line.

2. Flip the triangles open and press toward the light blue. Measure and trim to be sure the units are 3½" square.

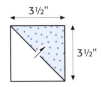

Make 12.

Making the Boat Hulls

1. Using a pencil and your rotary-cutting ruler, draw a diagonal line from corner to corner on the wrong side of the 2½" light blue print squares. Place a marked square on each end of a yellow rectangle, right sides together, as shown. Stitch along the pencil lines. Repeat to make 12 rectangles with a light blue print square on each corner.

 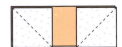

2. Align the ¼" line of a rotary-cutting ruler along the seam line of each square and trim away the excess fabric. Flip open the triangles and press toward the blue.

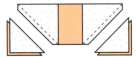 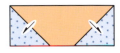

Make 12.

Making the Blocks

1. Assemble the pieces for each block as shown. Make 12 Sailboat blocks. I made 6 blocks with the large sail on the right and 6 blocks with the large sail on the left.

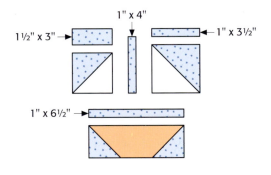

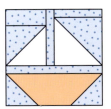 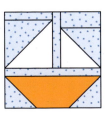

Make 6 with large sail on right.   Make 6 with large sail on left.

2. Cut the blue cloud rectangles once on the diagonal as follows. With the fabric right side up, cut 14 rectangles in half to yield 28 triangles that angle in one direction. Label this set of triangles stack A. With the fabric right side down, cut 10 rectangles to yield 20 triangles that angle in the opposite direction. Label this set of triangles stack B.

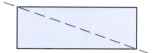

Stack A
Cut 14 rectangles in half
with fabric right side up.

Stack B
Cut 10 rectangles in half
with fabric right side down.

3. Take a triangle from stack A. Align the long, bias edge (the cut edge) of the triangle with a Sailboat block, extending the wide end of the triangle slightly beyond the block's edge. Stitch from the wide end to the narrow end, pressing the seam allowance toward the triangle. Using triangles from stack A, stitch a triangle to each remaining edge in the same manner. Make 7 blocks.

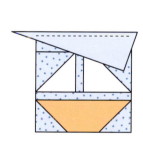
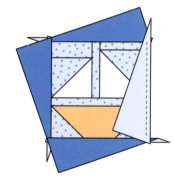

Using triangles from stack B, make 5 blocks that tilt in the opposite direction.

Block A
Make 7.

Block B
Make 5.

Assembling the Quilt

Measure your Sailboat blocks, referring to "Squaring Up the Blocks" on page 16, to make sure the blocks are sized consistently. You may need to trim the setting squares to match.

1. Arrange the blocks in rows, alternating the pieced blocks with the setting squares.

2. Sew the blocks together in rows, pressing the seams toward the setting squares.

3. Sew the rows together, pressing the seams all in one direction.

Adding the Borders

Refer to "Borders" on pages 18–19 for more details, if needed. Measure the quilt through the center and cut the border strips to fit that measurement.

1. Sew the inner borders to the sides of the quilt. Press toward the border.

2. Sew the inner borders to the top and bottom of the quilt. Press.

3. Repeat with the outer borders, pressing toward the outer border.

Finishing the Quilt

Refer to the general directions, beginning with "Preparing to Quilt" on page 19, for more details on quilting and finishing.

1. Cut the backing fabric so it is approximately 4" to 6" larger than the quilt top.

2. Layer the backing, batting, and quilt top, and baste the layers together.

3. Hand or machine quilt as desired. The quilt shown was machine quilted with sunbursts in the setting squares, curves in the sailboat blocks, and waves in the borders.

4. Trim the batting and backing fabric so the edges are even with the quilt-top edges, and bind the quilt. Add a hanging sleeve, if desired, and a label.

BABY BASKETS

My granddaughter, the owner of this quilt, loves to stroke the leaves with her fingers, but she spends most of her time on or under the "Little Buddy" companion quilt, shown on page 56. I whizzed that one together when I realized she needed one quilt to gaze at and another one to hold.

Materials

All yardages are based on 42"-wide fabric unless otherwise stated.

1¼ yds. light green for setting blocks and outer border

¾ yd. white for block background

⅝ yd. medium green for baskets, inner borders, and leaves

½ yd. medium peach for baskets and flowers

⅛ yd. (or scraps) of accent green for baskets and leaves

⅛ yd. light peach or scraps for baskets and flowers

1⅜ yds. fabric for backing

⅜ yd. fabric for binding

39" x 39" batting

Cutting

Fabric	Used For	First Cut	Second Cut	Third Cut
White	Block background	1 strip, 6" x 42"	5 squares, 6" x 6"	Cut once diagonally to make 10 triangles; use 9.
		1 strip, 3½" x 21"	5 squares, 3½" x 3½"	Cut once diagonally to make 10 triangles; use 9.
		2 strips, 1¾" x 42" 1 strip, 1¾" x 21" 1 strip, 2¼" x 42"	18 rectangles, 1¾" x 4¼" 9 squares, 1¾" x 1¾" 18 squares, 2¼" x 2¼"	— — —
Medium peach	Baskets	2 strips, 2¼" x 42"	20 squares, 2¼" x 2¼"	Cut 10 once diagonally to make 20 triangles.
	Handles	5 bias strips, 1" x 10"	—	—
Medium green	Baskets	1 strip, 2¼" x 42"	16 squares, 2¼" x 2¼"	Cut 8 once diagonally to make 16 triangles.
	Inner border*	4 strips, 1½" x 42"	2 strips, 1½" x 27" 2 strips, 1½" x 29"	— —
	Handles	4 bias strips, 1" x 10"	—	—
Accent green	Basket centers	2 squares, 3½" x 3½"	Cut once diagonally to make 4 triangles.	—
Light peach	Basket centers	3 squares, 3½" x 3½"	Cut once diagonally to make 6 triangles.	—
Light green	Setting squares	1 strip, 6¾" x 42"	4 squares, 6¾" x 6¾"	—
	Setting triangles	2 squares, 10¼" x 10¼"	Cut twice diagonally to make 8 triangles.	—
	Corner triangles	2 squares, 5½" x 5½"	Cut once diagonally to make 4 triangles.	—
	Outer border*	4 strips, 3½" x 42"	2 strips, 3½" x 29" 2 strips, 3½" x 35"	— —

* Wait until you have completed the center of the quilt before making the second cut for borders. Measure the quilt through the center and cut the border strips to fit that measurement.

QUILT SIZE: 34½" x 34½" • BLOCK SIZE: 6¼"

Designed and pieced by Mary Hickey. Quilted by Dawn Kelly.

Making the Block Units

1. Layer 10 white 2¼" squares with 10 medium peach 2¼" squares in pairs, right sides together, with the white square on top. Using a pencil and your rotary-cutting ruler, draw a diagonal line through the center of the white square. Draw a second line ¼" to the left of the first line. Draw a third line ¼" to the right of the first line.

2. Layer 8 of the white 2¼" squares with 8 of the medium green 2¼" squares in pairs, right sides together, with the white squares on top. Using a pencil and your rotary-cutting ruler, draw a diagonal line through the center of the white square as shown. Draw a second line ¼" to the left of the first line. Draw a third line ¼" to the right of the first line.

3. Stitch along the second and third lines of all the pairs. Cut along the first line.

4. Flip the triangles open and press toward the darker fabric. Measure and trim the units to 1¾" square. Make 20 peach-and-white squares and 16 green-and-white squares.

Make 20.   Make 16.

Assembling the Blocks

1. Arrange the units made in the preceding section with the center triangle, the small triangles, and the 1¾" background square to form the blocks, as shown. Stitch the pieces together starting with the small triangles and triangle-square sections.

2. Stitch the background rectangles to the remaining basket triangles, as shown.

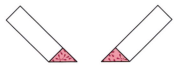

3. Stitch the rectangle units to the basket units made in step 1.

4. Sew the smaller background triangle to the bottom of each basket. Using a long stitch length, sew the large triangle to the top of each basket.

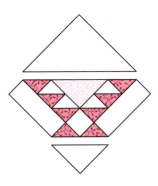

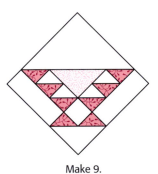

Make 9.

Making the Basket Handles

1. Press under ¼" on each side of the 1" x 10" bias strips.

2. Pin the bias strip onto the basket triangle in a smooth arc, using the placement diagram on page 83 as a guide. Leave at least ¼" extra at each end where the handle joins the basket.

3. Appliqué by hand or machine. See "Appliqué Primer" on pages 13–16 for further details, if needed.

4. Use a seam ripper to gently open the seam between the basket and the large white triangle. Trim the ends of the basket handle to ¼" if necessary and tuck them into the seam. Whip stitch the seam closed.

Assembling the Quilt

1. Arrange the blocks, setting squares, and setting triangles in diagonal rows.

2. Sew the blocks together in diagonal rows, pressing the seams toward the setting blocks.

3. Sew the rows together, pressing the seams all in one direction.

4. Trim and square up the quilt center along the edges as needed.

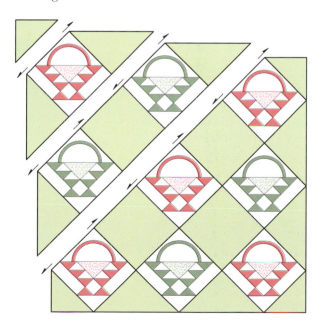

Making the Leaves and Flowers

1. Make templates of the leaf, flower, and flower center using the patterns on page 83.

2. Cut 30 leaves from the green scraps, adding ¼" around the edges for the seam allowance.

3. Layer the leaves right sides together in pairs.

4. Using a tiny stitch, sew ¼" from the edge around the leaf shapes. Leave the bottom of the leaf open. Trim the seam allowance to a scant ⅛".

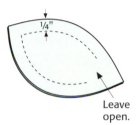

Leave open.

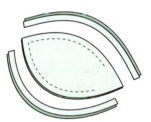

Trim seam allowance to ⅛".

5. Turn each leaf right side out and press, making a small pleat in the bottom of the leaf.

6. Tack the bottoms of the leaves in place, by hand or machine. Place them on 5 of the blocks. Refer to the quilt photograph on page 79 for placement.

7. Decide which appliqué method you will use (face-and-turn, fusible, or needle turn) and cut 5 flower shapes from the medium peach fabric using the flower template. Cut the flower centers from the light peach fabric or from scraps.

8. Use your chosen appliqué method to appliqué the flowers to the blocks, being careful to cover the raw ends of the leaves. See "Appliqué Primer" on pages 13–16 for more details, if needed.

9. Tack the tips of the leaves to the blocks and setting squares.

Adding the Borders

Refer to "Borders" on pages 18–19 for more details, if needed. Measure the quilt through the center and cut the border strips to fit that measurement.

1. Sew the inner borders to the sides of the quilt. Press toward the border.

2. Sew the inner borders to the top and bottom of the quilt. Press.

3. Repeat with the outer borders, pressing toward the outer border.

Finishing the Quilt

Refer to the general directions, beginning with "Preparing to Quilt" on page 19, for more details on quilting and finishing.

1. Cut the backing fabric so it is approximately 4" to 6" larger than the quilt top.

2. Layer the backing, batting, and quilt top, and baste the layers together.

3. Hand or machine quilt as desired. The quilt shown was machine quilted with outlines and curves in the blocks, echo quilting around the appliqué, jaunty flowers in the setting squares and leaves in the borders.

4. Trim the batting and backing fabric so the edges are even with the quilt-top edges, and bind the quilt. Add a hanging sleeve, if desired, and a label.

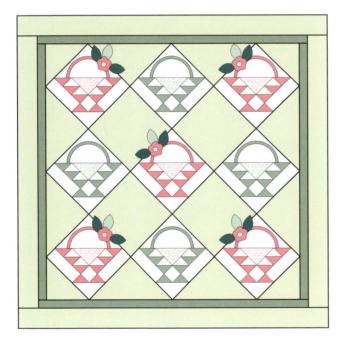

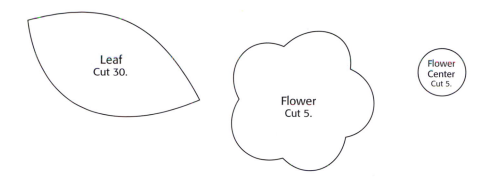

Leaf
Cut 30.

Flower
Cut 5.

Flower
Center
Cut 5.

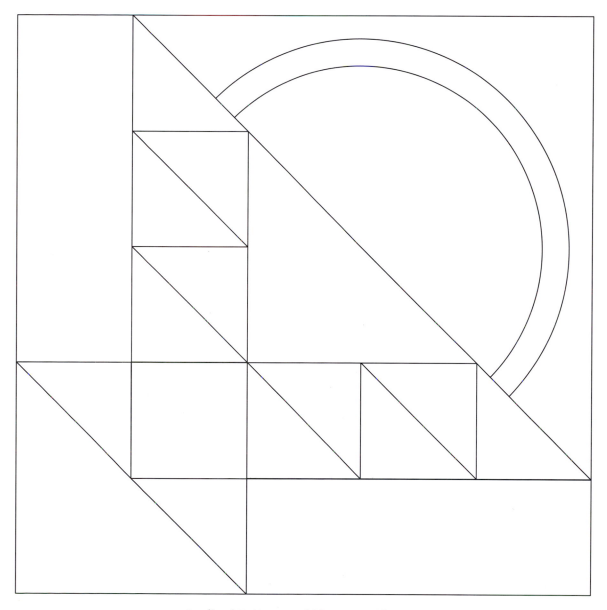

Appliqué Patterns and Placement Diagram

PIPSQUEAK PICNIC

This block really brings out the best in a special fabric. It can showcase a dignified toile or any conversation or novelty print. Although this quilt uses triangles to frame the sweet little scenes of children playing outdoors, you never have to cut or hold a small triangle. In this quilt, a monochromatic palette emphasizes the playful scenes in the toile fabric.

Materials

All yardages are based on 42"-wide fabric.

⅞ yd. dark blue for blocks, sashing, and outer border

¾ yd. white-and-blue toile for block centers

⅝ yd. light blue for sashing and inner border

½ yd. white-and-blue print for block background

¼ yd. medium blue for corners of the blocks

1½ yds. fabric for backing

⅜ yd. fabric for binding

40" x 40" batting

Mary's Helpful Hint

The center section of the block finishes at 5". I like to use my 6" bias square ruler and a blue water-soluble pen to mark the cuts that I plan, especially if I have only a small amount of toile or novelty fabric. I mark all the "fussy" cuts on the fabric first, then cut the 5½" squares.

Cutting

Fabric	Used For	Number to Cut	Size to Cut	Second Cut
Dark blue	Triangles in blocks, sashing, and border squares	3 strips	2" x 42"	44 squares, 2" x 2" (36 for the blocks and 8 for sashing and inner borders)
	Outer triangles in blocks	3 strips	1½" x 42"	72 squares, 1½" x 1½"
	Outer border*	4 strips	3½" x 42"	4 strips, 3½" x 30½"
White-and-blue toile	Centers of the blocks	9 squares	5½" x 5½"	—
White-and-blue print	Block background	6 strips	2" x 42"	72 rectangles, 2" x 3"
Medium blue	Block corner squares	2 strips	2" x 42"	36 squares, 2" x 2"
Light blue	Sashing	3 strips	2" x 42"	12 rectangles, 2" x 8½"
	Inner border*	4 strips	2" x 42"	4 strips, 2" x 27½"
	Outer border corner squares	4 squares	3½" x 3½"	—

* Wait until you have completed the center of the quilt before making the second cut for borders. Measure the quilt through the center and cut the border strips to fit that measurement.

QUILT SIZE: 36" x 36" • BLOCK SIZE: 8"

Designed by Mary Hickey. Pieced by Cleo Nollette; quilted by Dawn Kelly.

Making the Blocks

1. Using a pencil and your rotary-cutting ruler, draw a diagonal line from corner to corner on the wrong side of 36 of the dark blue 2" squares. Place a marked square on each corner of a 5½" toile square, right sides together. Stitch along the pencil lines. Repeat to make a total of 9 squares with a blue square on each corner.

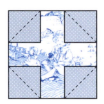

2. Align the ¼" line of a rotary-cutting ruler along the seam line of each square and trim away the excess fabric. Flip open the triangles and press toward the dark blue.

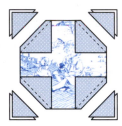

Make 9.

3. Using a pencil and your rotary-cutting ruler, draw a diagonal line from corner to corner on the wrong side of the 72 dark blue 1½" squares. Place a marked square on one corner of a 2" x 3" background rectangle, taking care to orient your marked squares as shown. Stitch along the pencil lines. Make 36 rectangle units with a square on the left and 36 with a square on the right.

4. Align the ¼" line of a rotary-cutting ruler along the seam line of each unit and trim away the excess

fabric. Flip open the remaining triangles and press toward the dark blue.

Make 36.

Make 36.

5. Stitch each pair of rectangles into a unit with blue triangles meeting in the middle. Press the seams open to minimize bulk.

Make 36.

6. Sew a medium blue square to each end of 18 of the rectangle units. Press toward the blue squares.

7. Arrange the units to form the blocks, as shown. Make 9 blocks.

Make 9.

Assembling the Quilt

1. Arrange the blocks in rows, with sashing strips between them. Sew the blocks together in 3 rows of 3 blocks, pressing the seams toward the blocks.

Make 3.

2. Stitch 3 sashing strips together with 2" dark blue squares between them. Press the seams toward the dark blue squares. Repeat to make 2 of these units.

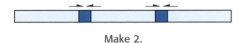

Make 2.

3. Sew the rows together with the sashing units. Press the seams all in one direction.

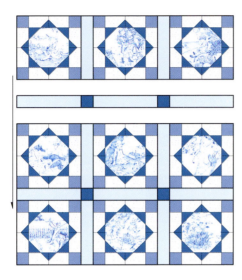

Adding the Borders

Refer to "Borders" on pages 18–19 for more details, if needed. Be sure to measure the quilt top through the center and cut the border strips to fit that measurement.

1. Sew an inner border strip to each side of the quilt. Press the seams toward the border.

2. Stitch 2" dark blue squares to the ends of the remaining light blue border strips. Press toward the light blue strips.

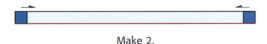

Make 2.

3. Sew the inner border units to the top and bottom of the quilt. Press.

4. Stitch the dark blue outer border strips to the sides of the quilt. Press toward the outer border.

5. Sew the light blue squares to the ends of the remaining dark blue border strips.

6. Sew the border units to the top and bottom of the quilt. Press.

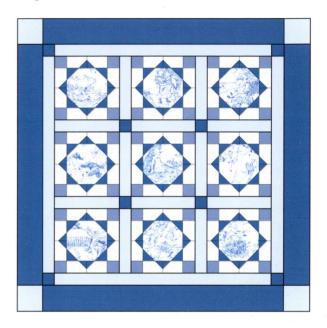

Finishing the Quilt

Refer to the general directions, beginning with "Preparing to Quilt" on page 19, for more details on quilting and finishing.

1. Cut the backing fabric so it is approximately 4" to 6" larger than the quilt top.

2. Layer the backing, batting, and quilt top, and baste the layers together.

3. Hand or machine quilt as desired. The quilt shown was machine quilted with scallops around the blocks and a double loop design in the border.

4. Trim the batting and backing fabric so the edges are even with the quilt-top edges, and bind the quilt. Add a hanging sleeve, if desired, and a label.

EVENING STARS

Delicate greens and soft blues create a soothing wash of color in this appealing quilt made of two pieced blocks. The light green bands in the Double Snowball blocks link with the light blue backgrounds between the Evening Star points to create a graceful wash of color, soothing and pleasant. By making the quilt with many scrap fabrics you can add interest and transparency. The blocks are constructed of simple folded corners—no fussing with triangles.

Materials

All yardages are based on 42"-wide fabric unless otherwise stated.

1 yd. light green or scraps for Double Snowball block centers and outer border

⅝ yd. white-and-green print or scraps for bands in Double Snowball block

½ yd. light blue or scraps for star corners and inner border

½ yd. dark blue or scraps for star points

⅜ yd. white-and-blue print or scraps for Star block background

⅜ yd. medium blue or scraps for centers of the Star blocks

¼ yd. dark green or scraps for Double Snowball block corners

1¾ yds. fabric for backing
½ yd. fabric for binding
42" x 42" batting

Making the Star Blocks

1. Using a pencil and your rotary-cutting ruler, draw a diagonal line from corner to corner on the wrong side of the dark blue squares. Place a marked square on one end of a white-and-blue rectangle as shown, right sides together. Stitch along the pencil lines. Align the ¼" line of a rotary-cutting ruler along the seam line of the square and trim away the excess fabric. Flip open the triangle and press toward the dark blue.

Cutting

Fabric	Used For	Number to Cut	Size to Cut	Second Cut
Dark blue	Points of Star blocks	6 strips	2" x 42"	104 squares, 2" x 2"
White-and-green print	Bands in Double Snowball blocks	5 strips	3½" x 42"	48 squares, 3½" x 3½"
White-and-blue print	Star block background	5 strips	2" x 42"	52 rectangles, 2" x 3½"
Medium blue	Centers of Star blocks	2 strips	3½" x 42"	13 squares, 3½" x 3½"
Light blue	Corners of Star blocks	3 strips	2" x 42"	52 squares, 2" x 2"
	Inner border*	4 strips	1½" x 42"	2 strips, 1½" x 30½" 2 strips, 1½" x 32½"
Light green	Double Snowball block centers	2 strips	6½" x 42"	12 squares, 6½" x 6½"
	Outer border*	4 strips	3½" x 42"	2 strips, 3½" x 32½" 2 strips, 3½" x 38½"
Dark green	Outer corners of Double Snowball blocks	3 strips	2" x 42"	48 squares, 2" x 2"

* Wait until you have completed the center of the quilt before making the second cut for borders. Measure the quilt through the center and cut the border strips to fit that measurement.

QUILT SIZE: 38" x 38" • BLOCK SIZE: 6"

Designed and pieced by Mary Hickey. Quilted by Fannie Schwartz.

2. Place a marked square on the other end of the rectangle, right sides together, and stitch along the pencil line. Trim the excess fabric, flip open the triangle, and press toward the dark blue. Repeat to make 52 rectangles with a dark blue triangle at each end.

Make 52.

3. Arrange the pieces from step 2 with the medium blue center squares and light blue corner squares to form the blocks. Make 13 Star blocks.

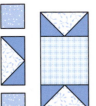 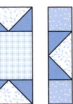 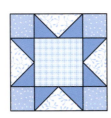

Make 13.

Making the Double Snowball Blocks

1. Using a pencil and your rotary-cutting ruler, draw a diagonal line from corner to corner on the wrong side of the white-and-green squares. Place marked squares on opposite corners of a light green square as shown, right sides together. Stitch along the pencil lines. Align the ¼" line of a rotary-cutting ruler along the seam line of each square and trim away the excess fabric. Flip open the triangles and press toward the light green square.

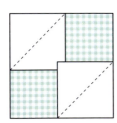 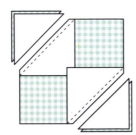

2. Place marked squares on the other two corners, right sides together. Stitch along the pencil lines. Trim the excess fabric, flip open the triangles, and press. Repeat to make 12 blocks with a white-and-green triangle on each corner.

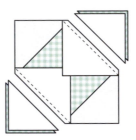 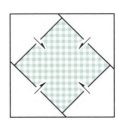

Make 12.

3. Using a pencil and your rotary-cutting ruler, draw a diagonal line from corner to corner on the wrong side of the dark green squares. Place a marked square on each corner of the green-and-white squares made in steps 1 and 2, right sides together, as shown. Stitch along the pencil lines. Repeat on all 12 blocks, adding a dark green triangle to each corner.

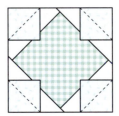

4. Align the ¼" line of a rotary-cutting ruler along the seam line of each square and trim away the excess fabric. Flip open the triangles and press toward the dark green.

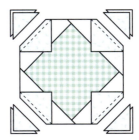 

Make 12.

To create the soft washed effect of this quilt, the point where the white-and-green print of the Double Snowball block meets the white-and-blue print of the Star blocks should match precisely. I find it necessary to pin or baste the points where the blocks match. I like to pin the points, run them through my machine with a very large stitch, and then check them. If they match nicely, I sew them with a regular size stitch—if not, I can easily rip them out and try again.

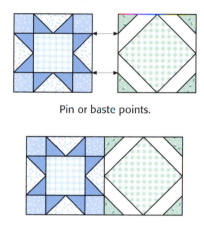

Pin or baste points.

Assembling the Quilt

1. Arrange the blocks in rows, alternating the blocks.

2. Sew the blocks together in rows, pressing the seams toward the Double Snowball blocks.

3. Sew the rows together, pressing the seams all in one direction.

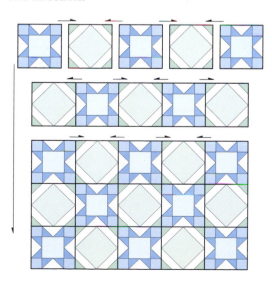

Adding the Borders

Refer to "Borders" on pages 18–19 for more details, if needed. Measure the quilt through the center and cut the border strips to fit that measurement.

1. Sew the inner borders to the sides of the quilt. Press toward the border.

2. Sew the inner borders to the top and bottom of the quilt. Press.

3. Repeat with the outer borders, pressing toward the outer border.

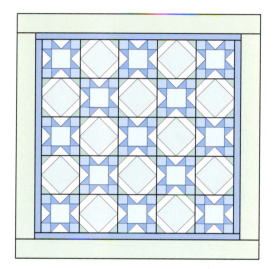

Finishing the Quilt

Refer to the general directions, beginning with "Preparing to Quilt" on page 19, for more details on quilting and finishing.

1. Cut the backing fabric so it is approximately 4" to 6" larger than the quilt top.

2. Layer the backing, batting, and quilt top, and baste the layers together.

3. Hand or machine quilt as desired. The quilt shown was hand quilted with a small medallion in the centers of the blocks, in-the-ditch quilting in the rest of the blocks, and a ribbon design in the borders.

4. Trim the batting and backing fabric so the edges are even with the quilt-top edges, and bind the quilt. Add a hanging sleeve, if desired, and a label.

TOPSY TURVY HEARTS

This is an adorable quilt to welcome either a baby boy or a baby girl. By tilting each Heart block in a different direction and using a green-and-white stripe fabric in the lower corners, these sweet but hard-working hearts surprise us with a star in their midst. The Heart blocks are easily made with simple folded corners, and the star makes itself out of the lower corners of the Heart blocks. What talented little hearts!

Materials

All yardages are based on 42"-wide fabric unless otherwise stated.

¾ yd. medium pink for hearts and outer border
½ yd. pale pink for setting squares and triangles
⅜ yd. green-and-white stripe for corners of the hearts
¼ yd. white for block background
¼ yd. yellow for hearts

¼ yd. blue for hearts
¼ yd. dark pink for inner border
¼ yd. medium green for Square-within-a-Square blocks
¼ yd. light green for Square-within-a-Square blocks
1⅜ yds. fabric for backing
⅜ yd. fabric for binding
38" x 38" batting

Cutting

Fabric	Used For	Number to Cut	Size to Cut	Second Cut
White	Background of hearts	2 strips	1¼" x 42"	64 squares, 1¼" x 1¼"
		2 strips	1¼" x 42"	16 rectangles, 1¼" x 5"
Medium pink	Hearts	2 strips	2¾" x 42"	16 rectangles, 2¾" x 4¼"
	Outer border*	4 strips	3½" x 42"	2 strips, 3½" x 28"
				2 strips, 3½" x 34"
Yellow	Hearts	1 strip	2¾" x 42"	8 rectangles, 2¾" x 4¼"
Blue	Hearts	1 strip	2¾" x 42"	8 rectangles, 2¾" x 4¼"
Green-and-white stripe	Corners of hearts	3 strips	2¾" x 42"	32 squares, 2¾" x 2¾"
Medium green	Square-within-a-Square	2 strips	2¾" x 42"	16 squares, 2¾" x 2¾"
Light green	Square-within-a-Square	1 strip	5" x 42"	4 squares, 5" x 5"
Pale pink	Setting triangles	1 strip	7¾" x 42"	3 squares, 7¾" x 7¾"; cut twice diagonally to make 12 triangles.
	Setting squares	5 squares	5" x 5"	–
	Corner triangles	2 squares	4¼" x 4¼"	Cut once diagonally to make 4 triangles.
Dark pink	Inner border*	4 strips	1½" x 42"	2 strips, 1½" x 26"
				2 strips, 1½" x 28"

* Wait until you have completed the center of the quilt before making the second cut for borders. Measure the quilt through the center and cut the border strips to fit that measurement.

QUILT SIZE: 33½" x 33½" • BLOCK SIZE: 4½"

Designed and pieced by Mary Hickey. Quilted by Frankie Schmitt.

Making the Heart Blocks

1. Using a pencil and your rotary-cutting ruler, draw a diagonal line from corner to corner on the wrong side of the white squares. Place a marked square on 2 corners of each 2¾" x 4¼" pink, yellow, and blue rectangle as shown, right sides together, so that the diagonal lines run from the upper middle to the outer side edges of the rectangles.

2. Sew on the marked line. Repeat to make 32 units.

3. Align the ¼" line of a rotary-cutting ruler along the seam line of each unit and trim away the excess fabric. Flip open the remaining white triangles and press toward the triangle.

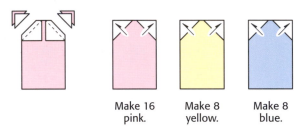

Make 16 pink.   Make 8 yellow.   Make 8 blue.

4. Draw a diagonal line from corner to corner on the wrong side of the green-and-white striped squares. Place a marked square on each 2¾" x 4¼" rectangle made in step 3, right sides together as shown. Note the direction of the stripes and the marked lines. For pink, position 8 squares with the diagonal line going from lower left to upper right, and 8 squares with the line going from lower right to upper left. For yellow and blue, there should be 4 squares with marked lines going in each direction. Sew on the marked lines. You will have a total of 16 pink units, 8 yellow units, and 8 blue units.

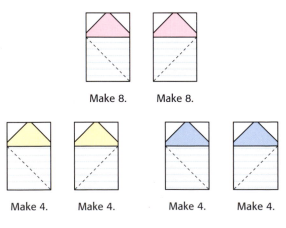

Make 8.   Make 8.

Make 4.   Make 4.   Make 4.   Make 4.

5. Align the ¼" line of a rotary-cutting ruler along the seam line of each unit and trim away the excess fabric. Flip open the remaining green-and-white striped triangles and press toward the rectangles.

6. Sew the units together to make 16 hearts.

7. Sew the white rectangles to the tops of the heart units from step 6 as shown. Make 16 blocks.

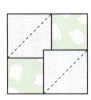

Making the Square-within-a-Square Blocks

1. Using a pencil and your rotary-cutting rule, draw a diagonal line from corner to corner on the wrong side of the medium green squares. Place marked squares on two opposite corners of a light green square, right sides together. Sew on the marked line. Align the ¼" line of a rotary-cutting ruler along the seam line of each unit and trim away the excess fabric. Flip open the triangles and press toward the medium green.

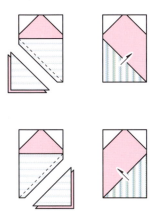

Mary Hickey has been an influential leader in the quilting world for more than twenty-five years. She continually brings new techniques, designs, and ideas to quiltmaking. When she was younger, she taught and lectured all over the world. Now she has turned her energies to creating fresh-looking quilts, clever techniques, and traditional patterns. She lives in the Northwestern coastal area of Washington state, where she thoroughly enjoys her family, especially her first grandchild, Audrey. Mary loves listening to baseball, opera, and books on tape while stitching on her porch overlooking Liberty Bay.

Mary's primary goal in designing, writing, and teaching is always the same: she wants to design projects and write directions that enable quiltmakers to create beautiful, traditional quilts that look complex, artistic, and stunning but that are easy to make.

ABOUT THE AUTHOR

❖ *96* ❖

2. Place marked squares on the other two corners, right sides together. Stitch along the pencil lines. Trim the excess fabric, flip open the triangles, and press. Make 4 Square-within-a-Square blocks.

Make 4.

Assembling the Quilt

1. Arrange the Heart blocks, the Square-within-a-Square blocks, the setting squares, and the setting triangles in diagonal rows. Pay special attention to correct positioning of the Heart blocks.

2. Sew the blocks together in diagonal rows, pressing the seams toward the Heart blocks.

3. Sew the rows together, pressing the seams all in one direction.

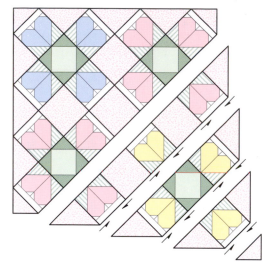

Adding the Borders

Refer to "Borders" on pages 18–19 for more details, if needed. Measure the quilt through the center and cut the border strips to fit that measurement.

1. Sew the inner borders to the sides of the quilt. Press toward the border.

2. Sew the inner borders to the top and bottom of the quilt. Press.

3. Repeat with the outer borders, pressing toward the outer border.

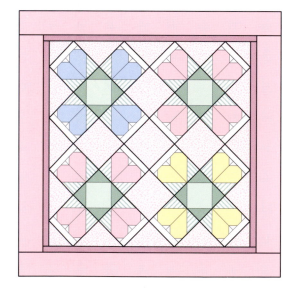

Finishing the Quilt

Refer to the general directions, beginning with "Preparing to Quilt" on page 19, for more details on quilting and finishing.

1. Cut the backing fabric so it is approximately 4" to 6" larger than the quilt top.

2. Layer the backing, batting, and quilt top, and baste the layers together.

3. Hand or machine quilt as desired. The quilt shown was machine quilted with outline quilting in the blocks, a delicate wreath in the pale pink setting squares, and a heart-and-loop design in the border.

4. Trim the batting and backing fabric so the edges are even with the quilt-top edges, and bind the quilt. Add a hanging sleeve, if desired, and a label.

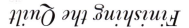